BIRDER'S
LIFE LIST & JOURNAL

The**Cornell**Lab of Ornithology

Published by Princeton University Press
41 William Street, Princeton, New Jersey 08540
6 Oxford Street, Woodstock, Oxfordshire OX20 1TR
press.princeton.edu

ISBN: 978-0-691-19471-4

Printed in China

PRINCETON
press.princeton.edu

CONTENTS

Wilson's
Warbler

FOREWORD

It was mid-winter of 2003 when I packed my office for the long-awaited move into the Cornell Lab of Ornithology's new home at Sapsucker Woods. Tucked among my collection of field books I came across an old, maroon-and-black notebook filled with notes by a young teenager in love with birds. Most were dated between 1964 and 1967—pencil-scrawled dates, locales, and descriptions of plumage and behavior. I flipped randomly through this cherished memento—my very first life list—and was immediately transported away from a snowy Ithaca, New York, to places and times where I had seen birds both ordinary and special. Most were in Minnesota. I relived my very first Wood Thrush (July 15, 1966), singing along forested railroad tracks overlooking the St. Croix River, and felt again my excitement at identifying a Piping Plover on the shore of Lake Pepin.

Keeping notes on birds we see preserves, for later enjoyment, our first glimpses and our wonderful experiences with these beautiful and mysterious creatures. But today, even more important reasons exist to keep a life list. As I thumbed through mine, I realized that among my notes about birds and places were some important records of change. On July 7, 1963, I noted a Red-headed Woodpecker "on a pine tree" at my home north of St. Paul. This was not an unusual sighting, as my notes for this species go on to read "regularly seen" at home. Today, however, Red-headed Woodpeckers are virtually unheard of in that area of Minnesota. Oak savannas have been engulfed by suburban sprawl all over the Upper Midwest, and the Red-headed Woodpecker has declined by 68 percent over its entire range since 1970. Besides reminding me when and where I first saw this remarkable species, my life list notes actually serve as a voucher for the study and analysis of changing populations.

Keeping bird lists can empower us to help keep birds from disappearing. Years of records from a particular place serve to demonstrate how important that place is for species that use it. Lists take on broader importance when combined with lists kept by others. This is the concept behind citizen science as practiced by many of the Lab of Ornithology's programs. Findings from our citizen-science projects, such as eBird, have documented changes in bird populations over time and have appeared in some of the world's most prestigious scientific journals. Your involvement in the understanding and protection of birds might begin with a simple entry into a life list and expand to keeping regular lists at **eBird.org** for use in science and conservation. Your contributions to citizen-science projects are more important than ever before, as we learn how to cope with the enormous changes to our environment brought about by climate change and what these changes mean for the survival of many bird species.

We designed our *Birder's Life List and Journal* to make it easy for you to embark on your own journey to discovering more about birds. In this latest edition, we have also included open-ended pages with more space to allow for longer entries and sketches. By taking a few moments to jot down your observations, you will preserve for yourself—and perhaps for many others—the joy that bird watching brings, a joy that we hope will grow and last a lifetime.

John W. Fitzpatrick
Executive Director
Cornell Lab of Ornithology

Yellow Warblers

ABOUT THE
CORNELL LAB OF ORNITHOLOGY

Observing and keeping track of birds can be so rewarding. Let the Cornell Lab of Ornithology enrich your birding experiences with the following resources:

- Visit our All About Birds website (**AllAboutBirds.org**) to learn more about bird ID, bird sounds, behavior, nesting, and the kind of food and habitat a bird prefers.

- What is this bird? Solve the mystery with our free Merlin® Bird ID app by answering five questions, or with a photo of a bird. Merlin taps into the eBird database to reveal the list of birds that best match your description or photo based on your location and time of year. Pick your bird, then delve into more photos, sounds, and ID tips.

- Explore the world of bird behavior and diversity with the Macaulay Library (**MacaulayLibrary.org**) the world's premier scientific archive of natural-history audio, video, and photos contributed by citizen scientists from all over the globe. Find out what your bird looks like in its natural habitat, in male and female plumage, or listen to it sing.

- Keep track of your lists throughout the year with **eBird.org** to build a lifetime of memories while benefiting birds. Your observations in eBird are valuable data that can be used by researchers, conservationists, and the birding community. Are you dreaming of finding that special bird? In addition to keeping track of your own sightings, you can tap into eBird to find birds that were last seen in your area, or anywhere in the world.

Ruby-throated
Hummingbird

- Check out Bird Academy (**Academy.AllAboutBirds.org**) for interactives, videos, field clips, articles, and more on a wide variety of topics, from the science of feathers, to identifying bird song, to bird behavior. Want to master identification of raptors, sparrows, or shorebirds? Enroll in our self-paced courses.

Last but not least, consider joining our vibrant community of bird lovers from all over the world. Help conserve the birds that touch our lives and enrich our planet by becoming a member of the Cornell Lab of Ornithology. Our mission is to interpret and conserve the earth's biological diversity through research, education, and citizen science focused on birds. Dedicated to advancing the understanding and protection of the natural world, the Cornell Lab joins with people from all walks of life to make new scientific discoveries, share insights, and galvanize conservation action. Members receive our beautiful *Living Bird* magazine. Visit **Birds.Cornell.edu** to learn more.

ABOUT THIS JOURNAL

Northern Cardinal

This new edition includes all species known
to occur in the United States and Canada,
including those that regularly appear in Hawaii.
The *Birder's Life List and Journal* is based on the eBird
taxonomy v2018 current with Clements v2018 (released 14 August
2018), which is itself current with the 59th supplement to the American
Ornithological Society's Checklist of North American Birds (July 2018).
Both common and scientific names are provided within the list. Please
keep in mind that due to changes in nomenclature, the names of some
species will not be the same as those listed in older field guides.

QUICK SEARCH GUIDE

To quickly find the pages where a group of birds is listed, align the
colored bars on this page to the matching tabs in the list.

SPECIES LISTINGS

The species lists have space for writing brief notes for each bird.
You can use this space for listing subspecies, or for brief remarks
on behavior, habitat, and time of day. All of the species are listed in
taxonomic order, the same order used in most field guides. Introduced
birds are indicated by (I) following the common name.

North American Species: This list consists of 767 native and introduced
bird species found regularly in North America north of Mexico.

Hawaiian Species: Here we list 64 native and introduced birds found
on the Hawaiian Islands. These species are Hawaiian birds occurring

naturally in Hawaii that are not already listed in our North American Species list. Therefore, some birds seen in Hawaii appear only in the North American Species list, so be sure to check there if you cannot find the bird you are looking for in Hawaii.

Accidental Species: These species appear very rarely in the United States and Canada but have been officially accepted by the Committee on Classification and Nomenclature of the American Ornithologists' Union. Note that lists of accidentals appear at the end of the North American and Hawaiian species lists, respectively.

Extinct Species: Here we provide a list of birds in the United States and Canada that are known to be extinct or that may be extinct.

CHECKLIST
This is a complete list of all the birds of the United States and Canada. Introduced, Hawaiian, and accidental species are indicated by (I), (H), and (A), respectively.

BIRD NOTES
Here is a set of blank entries with additional space for recording your more memorable bird moments or for sketching birds.

INDEX
All the species included in this book are listed here in alphabetical order.

Hermit Thrush

QUICK SEARCH GUIDE

Anseriformes	Waterfowl: Ducks, Geese & Swans
Galliformes	Chachalaca; Grouse, Quail & Allies
Phoenicopteriformes Podicipediformes	Flamingo Grebes
Columbiformes Cuculiformes	Pigeons & Doves Cuckoos
Caprimulgiformes	Nightjars & Allies; Swifts; Hummingbirds
Gruiformes	Rails, Gallinules & Allies; Limpkin; Cranes
Charadriiformes	Shorebirds: Stilts & Avocets; Oystercatchers; Plovers Sandpipers & Allies Skuas & Jaegers; Auks: Murres & Puffins; Gulls, Terns, & Skimmer
Phaethontiformes Gaviiformes	Tropicbirds Loons
Procellariiformes	Albatrosses; Storm-Petrels; Shearwaters & Petrels
Ciconiiformes Suliformes Pelecaniformes	Stork Frigatebirds; Boobies & Gannets; Anhinga; Cormorants Pelicans; Herons: Egrets & Bitterns; Ibises & Spoonbill
Cathartiformes Accipitriformes	Vultures Osprey, Kites, Hawks, Eagles
Strigiformes	Owls
Trogoniformes Coraciiformes Piciformes	Trogon Kingfishers Woodpeckers
Falconiformes	Falcons & Caracara
Psittaciformes	Parrots, Parakeets & Allies
Passeriformes	Tyrant Flycatchers: Pewees, Kingbirds & Allies; Tityras & Allies; Shrikes; Vireos
	Jays, Magpies, Crows & Ravens
	Larks; Martins & Swallows; Chickadees & Titmice
	Nuthatches; Treecreeper; Wrens; Gnatcatchers; Kinglets; Old World Flycatchers
	Thrushes & Allies; Mockingbirds & Thrashers; Starlings; Wagtails & Pipits; Waxwings
	Finches & Allies; Longspurs & Snow Buntings
	Sparrows: Juncos, Towhees
	Orioles, Blackbirds, Cowbirds, Grackles
	New World Warblers
	Cardinals, Grosbeaks & Allies; Tanagers & Allies; Old World Sparrows
Hawaiian Species	Species found only in Hawaii

Cooper's
Hawk

BLACK-BELLIED WHISTLING-DUCK
Dendrocygna autumnalis

Date:

Location:

Notes:

FULVOUS WHISTLING-DUCK
Dendrocygna bicolor

Date:

Location:

Notes:

EMPEROR GOOSE
Anser canagicus

Date:

Location:

Notes:

SNOW GOOSE
Anser caerulescens

Date:

Location:

Notes:

ROSS'S GOOSE
Anser rossii

Date:

Location:

Notes:

GREATER WHITE-FRONTED GOOSE
Anser albifrons

Date:

Location:

Notes:

TAIGA BEAN-GOOSE *Anser fabalis*	Date:	Location:
Notes:		

TUNDRA BEAN-GOOSE *Anser serrirostris*	Date:	Location:
Notes:		

BRANT *Branta bernicla*	Date:	Location:
Notes:		

CACKLING GOOSE *Branta hutchinsii*	Date:	Location:
Notes:		

CANADA GOOSE *Branta canadensis*	Date:	Location:
Notes:		

MUTE SWAN (I) *Cygnus olor*	Date:	Location:
Notes:		

TRUMPETER SWAN
Cygnus buccinator

Date:

Location:

Notes:

TUNDRA SWAN
Cygnus columbianus

Date:

Location:

Notes:

WHOOPER SWAN
Cygnus cygnus

Date:

Location:

Notes:

EGYPTIAN GOOSE (I)
Alopochen aegyptiaca

Date:

Location:

Notes:

MUSCOVY DUCK
Cairina moschata

Date:

Location:

Notes:

WOOD DUCK
Aix sponsa

Date:

Location:

Notes:

BLUE-WINGED TEAL
Spatula discors

Date:

Location:

Notes:

CINNAMON TEAL
Spatula cyanoptera

Date:

Location:

Notes:

NORTHERN SHOVELER
Spatula clypeata

Date:

Location:

Notes:

GADWALL
Mareca strepera

Date:

Location:

Notes:

EURASIAN WIGEON
Mareca penelope

Date:

Location:

Notes:

AMERICAN WIGEON
Mareca americana

Date:

Location:

Notes:

MALLARD *Anas platyrhynchos*	Date:	Location:
Notes:		

MEXICAN DUCK *Anas diazi*	Date:	Location:
Notes:		

AMERICAN BLACK DUCK *Anas rubripes*	Date:	Location:
Notes:		

MOTTLED DUCK *Anas fulvigula*	Date:	Location:
Notes:		

NORTHERN PINTAIL *Anas acuta*	Date:	Location:
Notes:		

GREEN-WINGED TEAL *Anas crecca*	Date:	Location:
Notes:		

CANVASBACK
Aythya valisineria

Date:

Location:

Notes:

REDHEAD
Aythya americana

Date:

Location:

Notes:

COMMON POCHARD
Aythya ferina

Date:

Location:

Notes:

RING-NECKED DUCK
Aythya collaris

Date:

Location:

Notes:

TUFTED DUCK
Aythya fuligula

Date:

Location:

Notes:

GREATER SCAUP
Aythya marila

Date:

Location:

Notes:

LESSER SCAUP
Aythya affinis

Date:

Location:

Notes:

STELLER'S EIDER
Polysticta stelleri

Date:

Location:

Notes:

SPECTACLED EIDER
Somateria fischeri

Date:

Location:

Notes:

KING EIDER
Somateria spectabilis

Date:

Location:

Notes:

COMMON EIDER
Somateria mollissima

Date:

Location:

Notes:

HARLEQUIN DUCK
Histrionicus histrionicus

Date:

Location:

Notes:

SURF SCOTER
Melanitta perspicillata

Date:

Location:

Notes:

WHITE-WINGED SCOTER
Melanitta deglandi

Date:

Location:

Notes:

BLACK SCOTER
Melanitta americana

Date:

Location:

Notes:

LONG-TAILED DUCK
Clangula hyemalis

Date:

Location:

Notes:

BUFFLEHEAD
Bucephala albeola

Date:

Location:

Notes:

COMMON GOLDENEYE
Bucephala clangula

Date:

Location:

Notes:

BARROW'S GOLDENEYE *Bucephala islandica*	Date:	Location:
Notes:		

SMEW *Mergellus albellus*	Date:	Location:
Notes:		

HOODED MERGANSER *Lophodytes cucullatus*	Date:	Location:
Notes:		

COMMON MERGANSER *Mergus merganser*	Date:	Location:
Notes:		

RED-BREASTED MERGANSER *Mergus serrator*	Date:	Location:
Notes:		

MASKED DUCK *Nomonyx dominicus*	Date:	Location:
Notes:		

RUDDY DUCK *Oxyura jamaicensis*	Date:	Location:

Notes:

Notes:

PLAIN CHACHALACA *Ortalis vetula*	Date:	Location:
Notes:		

MOUNTAIN QUAIL *Oreortyx pictus*	Date:	Location:
Notes:		

NORTHERN BOBWHITE *Colinus virginianus*	Date:	Location:
Notes:		

SCALED QUAIL *Callipepla squamata*	Date:	Location:
Notes:		

CALIFORNIA QUAIL *Callipepla californica*	Date:	Location:
Notes:		

GAMBEL'S QUAIL *Callipepla gambelii*	Date:	Location:
Notes:		

MONTEZUMA QUAIL *Cyrtonyx montezumae*	Date:	Location:
Notes:		

CHUKAR (I) *Alectoris chukar*	Date:	Location:
Notes:		

HIMALAYAN SNOWCOCK (I) *Tetraogallus himalayensis*	Date:	Location:
Notes:		

RING-NECKED PHEASANT (I) *Phasianus colchicus*	Date:	Location:
Notes:		

GRAY PARTRIDGE (I) *Perdix perdix*	Date:	Location:
Notes:		

RUFFED GROUSE *Bonasa umbellus*	Date:	Location:
Notes:		

GREATER SAGE-GROUSE *Centrocercus urophasianus*	Date:	Location:
Notes:		

GUNNISON SAGE-GROUSE *Centrocercus minimus*	Date:	Location:
Notes:		

SPRUCE GROUSE *Falcipennis canadensis*	Date:	Location:
Notes:		

WILLOW PTARMIGAN *Lagopus lagopus*	Date:	Location:
Notes:		

ROCK PTARMIGAN *Lagopus muta*	Date:	Location:
Notes:		

WHITE-TAILED PTARMIGAN *Lagopus leucura*	Date:	Location:
Notes:		

DUSKY GROUSE *Dendragapus obscurus*	Date:	Location:
Notes:		

SOOTY GROUSE *Dendragapus fuliginosus*	Date:	Location:
Notes:		

SHARP-TAILED GROUSE *Tympanuchus phasianellus*	Date:	Location:
Notes:		

GREATER PRAIRIE-CHICKEN *Tympanuchus cupido*	Date:	Location:
Notes:		

LESSER PRAIRIE-CHICKEN *Tympanuchus pallidicinctus*	Date:	Location:
Notes:		

WILD TURKEY *Meleagris gallopavo*	Date:	Location:
Notes:		

AMERICAN FLAMINGO
Phoenicopterus ruber

Date: Location:

Notes:

LEAST GREBE
Tachybaptus dominicus

Date: Location:

Notes:

PIED-BILLED GREBE
Podilymbus podiceps

Date: Location:

Notes:

HORNED GREBE
Podiceps auritus

Date: Location:

Notes:

RED-NECKED GREBE
Podiceps grisegena

Date: Location:

Notes:

EARED GREBE
Podiceps nigricollis

Date: Location:

Notes:

WESTERN GREBE *Aechmophorus occidentalis*	Date:	Location:
Notes:		

CLARK'S GREBE *Aechmophorus clarkii*	Date:	Location:
Notes:		

Notes:

ROCK PIGEON (I) *Columba livia*	Date:	Location:
Notes:		

WHITE-CROWNED PIGEON *Patagioenas leucocephala*	Date:	Location:
Notes:		

RED-BILLED PIGEON *Patagioenas flavirostris*	Date:	Location:
Notes:		

BAND-TAILED PIGEON *Patagioenas fasciata*	Date:	Location:
Notes:		

EURASIAN COLLARED-DOVE (I) *Streptopelia decaocto*	Date:	Location:
Notes:		

SPOTTED DOVE (I) *Streptopelia chinensis*	Date:	Location:
Notes:		

INCA DOVE
Columbina inca

Date:

Location:

Notes:

COMMON GROUND-DOVE
Columbina passerina

Date:

Location:

Notes:

RUDDY GROUND-DOVE
Columbina talpacoti

Date:

Location:

Notes:

WHITE-TIPPED DOVE
Leptotila verreauxi

Date:

Location:

Notes:

WHITE-WINGED DOVE
Zenaida asiatica

Date:

Location:

Notes:

MOURNING DOVE
Zenaida macroura

Date:

Location:

Notes:

SMOOTH-BILLED ANI
Crotophaga ani
Date:
Location:
Notes:

GROOVE-BILLED ANI
Crotophaga sulcirostris
Date:
Location:
Notes:

GREATER ROADRUNNER
Geococcyx californianus
Date:
Location:
Notes:

YELLOW-BILLED CUCKOO
Coccyzus americanus
Date:
Location:
Notes:

MANGROVE CUCKOO
Coccyzus minor
Date:
Location:
Notes:

BLACK-BILLED CUCKOO
Coccyzus erythropthalmus
Date:
Location:
Notes:

COMMON CUCKOO *Cuculus canorus*	Date:	Location:

Notes:

Notes:

LESSER NIGHTHAWK
Chordeiles acutipennis

Date:

Location:

Notes:

COMMON NIGHTHAWK
Chordeiles minor

Date:

Location:

Notes:

ANTILLEAN NIGHTHAWK
Chordeiles gundlachii

Date:

Location:

Notes:

COMMON PAURAQUE
Nyctidromus albicollis

Date:

Location:

Notes:

COMMON POORWILL
Phalaenoptilus nuttallii

Date:

Location:

Notes:

CHUCK-WILL'S-WIDOW
Antrostomus carolinensis

Date:

Location:

Notes:

BUFF-COLLARED NIGHTJAR *Antrostomus ridgwayi*	Date:	Location:
Notes:		

EASTERN WHIP-POOR-WILL *Antrostomus vociferus*	Date:	Location:
Notes:		

MEXICAN WHIP-POOR-WILL *Antrostomus arizonae*	Date:	Location:
Notes:		

BLACK SWIFT *Cypseloides niger*	Date:	Location:
Notes:		

CHIMNEY SWIFT *Chaetura pelagica*	Date:	Location:
Notes:		

VAUX'S SWIFT *Chaetura vauxi*	Date:	Location:
Notes:		

WHITE-THROATED SWIFT
Aeronautes saxatalis

Date:

Location:

Notes:

MEXICAN VIOLETEAR
Colibri thalassinus

Date:

Location:

Notes:

RIVOLI'S HUMMINGBIRD
Eugenes fulgens

Date:

Location:

Notes:

BLUE-THROATED HUMMINGBIRD
Lampornis clemenciae

Date:

Location:

Notes:

LUCIFER HUMMINGBIRD
Calothorax lucifer

Date:

Location:

Notes:

RUBY-THROATED HUMMINGBIRD
Archilochus colubris

Date:

Location:

Notes:

BLACK-CHINNED HUMMINGBIRD *Archilochus alexandri*	Date:	Location:
Notes:		

ANNA'S HUMMINGBIRD *Calypte anna*	Date:	Location:
Notes:		

COSTA'S HUMMINGBIRD *Calypte costae*	Date:	Location:
Notes:		

BROAD-TAILED HUMMINGBIRD *Selasphorus platycercus*	Date:	Location:
Notes:		

RUFOUS HUMMINGBIRD *Selasphorus rufus*	Date:	Location:
Notes:		

ALLEN'S HUMMINGBIRD *Selasphorus sasin*	Date:	Location:
Notes:		

HUMMINGBIRDS

CALLIOPE HUMMINGBIRD
Selasphorus calliope

Date:

Location:

Notes:

BROAD-BILLED HUMMINGBIRD
Cynanthus latirostris

Date:

Location:

Notes:

BERYLLINE HUMMINGBIRD
Amazilia beryllina

Date:

Location:

Notes:

BUFF-BELLIED HUMMINGBIRD
Amazilia yucatanensis

Date:

Location:

Notes:

VIOLET-CROWNED HUMMINGBIRD
Amazilia violiceps

Date:

Location:

Notes:

WHITE-EARED HUMMINGBIRD
Hylocharis leucotis

Date:

Location:

Notes:

RIDGWAY'S RAIL
Rallus obsoletus

Date:

Location:

Notes:

KING RAIL
Rallus elegans

Date:

Location:

Notes:

CLAPPER RAIL
Rallus crepitans

Date:

Location:

Notes:

VIRGINIA RAIL
Rallus limicola

Date:

Location:

Notes:

SORA
Porzana carolina

Date:

Location:

Notes:

COMMON GALLINULE
Gallinula galeata

Date:

Location:

Notes:

AMERICAN COOT
Fulica americana

Date:

Location:

Notes:

PURPLE GALLINULE
Porphyrio martinica

Date:

Location:

Notes:

GRAY-HEADED SWAMPHEN
Porphyrio poliocephalus

Date:

Location:

Notes:

YELLOW RAIL
Coturnicops noveboracensis

Date:

Location:

Notes:

BLACK RAIL
Laterallus jamaicensis

Date:

Location:

Notes:

LIMPKIN
Aramus guarauna

Date:

Location:

Notes:

SANDHILL CRANE *Antigone canadensis*	Date:	Location:

Notes:

WHOOPING CRANE *Grus americana*	Date:	Location:

Notes:

Notes:

BLACK-NECKED STILT
Himantopus mexicanus

Date:

Location:

Notes:

AMERICAN AVOCET
Recurvirostra americana

Date:

Location:

Notes:

AMERICAN OYSTERCATCHER
Haematopus palliatus

Date:

Location:

Notes:

BLACK OYSTERCATCHER
Haematopus bachmani

Date:

Location:

Notes:

BLACK-BELLIED PLOVER
Pluvialis squatarola

Date:

Location:

Notes:

AMERICAN GOLDEN-PLOVER
Pluvialis dominica

Date:

Location:

Notes:

PACIFIC GOLDEN-PLOVER *Pluvialis fulva*	Date:	Location:
Notes:		

LESSER SAND-PLOVER *Charadrius mongolus*	Date:	Location:
Notes:		

SNOWY PLOVER *Charadrius nivosus*	Date:	Location:
Notes:		

WILSON'S PLOVER *Charadrius wilsonia*	Date:	Location:
Notes:		

COMMON RINGED PLOVER *Charadrius hiaticula*	Date:	Location:
Notes:		

SEMIPALMATED PLOVER *Charadrius semipalmatus*	Date:	Location:
Notes:		

PIPING PLOVER *Charadrius melodus*	Date:	Location:
Notes:		

KILLDEER *Charadrius vociferus*	Date:	Location:
Notes:		

MOUNTAIN PLOVER *Charadrius montanus*	Date:	Location:
Notes:		

UPLAND SANDPIPER *Bartramia longicauda*	Date:	Location:
Notes:		

BRISTLE-THIGHED CURLEW *Numenius tahitiensis*	Date:	Location:
Notes:		

WHIMBREL *Numenius phaeopus*	Date:	Location:
Notes:		

LONG-BILLED CURLEW
Numenius americanus

Date:

Location:

Notes:

BAR-TAILED GODWIT
Limosa lapponica

Date:

Location:

Notes:

BLACK-TAILED GODWIT
Limosa limosa

Date:

Location:

Notes:

HUDSONIAN GODWIT
Limosa haemastica

Date:

Location:

Notes:

MARBLED GODWIT
Limosa fedoa

Date:

Location:

Notes:

RUDDY TURNSTONE
Arenaria interpres

Date:

Location:

Notes:

BLACK TURNSTONE
Arenaria melanocephala

Date:

Location:

Notes:

RED KNOT
Calidris canutus

Date:

Location:

Notes:

SURFBIRD
Calidris virgata

Date:

Location:

Notes:

RUFF
Calidris pugnax

Date:

Location:

Notes:

SHARP-TAILED SANDPIPER
Calidris acuminata

Date:

Location:

Notes:

STILT SANDPIPER
Calidris himantopus

Date:

Location:

Notes:

CURLEW SANDPIPER *Calidris ferruginea*	Date:	Location:
Notes:		

TEMMINCK'S STINT *Calidris temminckii*	Date:	Location:
Notes:		

LONG-TOED STINT *Calidris subminuta*	Date:	Location:
Notes:		

RED-NECKED STINT *Calidris ruficollis*	Date:	Location:
Notes:		

SANDERLING *Calidris alba*	Date:	Location:
Notes:		

DUNLIN *Calidris alpina*	Date:	Location:
Notes:		

ROCK SANDPIPER
Calidris ptilocnemis

Date:

Location:

Notes:

PURPLE SANDPIPER
Calidris maritima

Date:

Location:

Notes:

BAIRD'S SANDPIPER
Calidris bairdii

Date:

Location:

Notes:

LEAST SANDPIPER
Calidris minutilla

Date:

Location:

Notes:

WHITE-RUMPED SANDPIPER
Calidris fuscicollis

Date:

Location:

Notes:

BUFF-BREASTED SANDPIPER
Calidris subruficollis

Date:

Location:

Notes:

PECTORAL SANDPIPER *Calidris melanotos*	Date:	Location:
Notes:		

SEMIPALMATED SANDPIPER *Calidris pusilla*	Date:	Location:
Notes:		

WESTERN SANDPIPER *Calidris mauri*	Date:	Location:
Notes:		

SHORT-BILLED DOWITCHER *Limnodromus griseus*	Date:	Location:
Notes:		

LONG-BILLED DOWITCHER *Limnodromus scolopaceus*	Date:	Location:
Notes:		

AMERICAN WOODCOCK *Scolopax minor*	Date:	Location:
Notes:		

	COMMON SNIPE *Gallinago gallinago*	Date:	Location:
Notes:			

	WILSON'S SNIPE *Gallinago delicata*	Date:	Location:
Notes:			

	TEREK SANDPIPER *Xenus cinereus*	Date:	Location:
Notes:			

	WILSON'S PHALAROPE *Phalaropus tricolor*	Date:	Location:
Notes:			

	RED-NECKED PHALAROPE *Phalaropus lobatus*	Date:	Location:
Notes:			

	RED PHALAROPE *Phalaropus fulicarius*	Date:	Location:
Notes:			

COMMON SANDPIPER *Actitis hypoleucos*	Date:	Location:
Notes:		

SPOTTED SANDPIPER *Actitis macularius*	Date:	Location:
Notes:		

SOLITARY SANDPIPER *Tringa solitaria*	Date:	Location:
Notes:		

GRAY-TAILED TATTLER *Tringa brevipes*	Date:	Location:
Notes:		

WANDERING TATTLER *Tringa incana*	Date:	Location:
Notes:		

GREATER YELLOWLEGS *Tringa melanoleuca*	Date:	Location:
Notes:		

COMMON GREENSHANK *Tringa nebularia*	Date:	Location:
Notes:		

WILLET *Tringa semipalmata*	Date:	Location:
Notes:		

LESSER YELLOWLEGS *Tringa flavipes*	Date:	Location:
Notes:		

WOOD SANDPIPER *Tringa glareola*	Date:	Location:
Notes:		

GREAT SKUA *Stercorarius skua*	Date:	Location:
Notes:		

SOUTH POLAR SKUA *Stercorarius maccormicki*	Date:	Location:
Notes:		

POMARINE JAEGER *Stercorarius pomarinus*	Date:	Location:
Notes:		

PARASITIC JAEGER *Stercorarius parasiticus*	Date:	Location:
Notes:		

LONG-TAILED JAEGER *Stercorarius longicaudus*	Date:	Location:
Notes:		

DOVEKIE *Alle alle*	Date:	Location:
Notes:		

COMMON MURRE *Uria aalge*	Date:	Location:
Notes:		

THICK-BILLED MURRE *Uria lomvia*	Date:	Location:
Notes:		

RAZORBILL *Alca torda*	Date:	Location:
Notes:		

BLACK GUILLEMOT *Cepphus grylle*	Date:	Location:
Notes:		

PIGEON GUILLEMOT *Cepphus columba*	Date:	Location:
Notes:		

LONG-BILLED MURRELET *Brachyramphus perdix*	Date:	Location:
Notes:		

MARBLED MURRELET *Brachyramphus marmoratus*	Date:	Location:
Notes:		

KITTLITZ'S MURRELET *Brachyramphus brevirostris*	Date:	Location:
Notes:		

SCRIPPS'S MURRELET *Synthliboramphus scrippsi*	Date:	Location:
Notes:		

GUADALUPE MURRELET *Synthliboramphus hypoleucus*	Date:	Location:
Notes:		

CRAVERI'S MURRELET *Synthliboramphus craveri*	Date:	Location:
Notes:		

ANCIENT MURRELET *Synthliboramphus antiquus*	Date:	Location:
Notes:		

CASSIN'S AUKLET *Ptychoramphus aleuticus*	Date:	Location:
Notes:		

PARAKEET AUKLET *Aethia psittacula*	Date:	Location:
Notes:		

LEAST AUKLET
Aethia pusilla

Date:

Location:

Notes:

WHISKERED AUKLET
Aethia pygmaea

Date:

Location:

Notes:

CRESTED AUKLET
Aethia cristatella

Date:

Location:

Notes:

RHINOCEROS AUKLET
Cerorhinca monocerata

Date:

Location:

Notes:

ATLANTIC PUFFIN
Fratercula arctica

Date:

Location:

Notes:

HORNED PUFFIN
Fratercula corniculata

Date:

Location:

Notes:

TUFTED PUFFIN *Fratercula cirrhata*	Date:	Location:
Notes:		

BLACK-LEGGED KITTIWAKE *Rissa tridactyla*	Date:	Location:
Notes:		

RED-LEGGED KITTIWAKE *Rissa brevirostris*	Date:	Location:
Notes:		

IVORY GULL *Pagophila eburnea*	Date:	Location:
Notes:		

SABINE'S GULL *Xema sabini*	Date:	Location:
Notes:		

BONAPARTE'S GULL *Chroicocephalus philadelphia*	Date:	Location:
Notes:		

BLACK-HEADED GULL
Chroicocephalus ridibundus

Date:

Location:

Notes:

LITTLE GULL
Hydrocoloeus minutus

Date:

Location:

Notes:

ROSS'S GULL
Rhodostethia rosea

Date:

Location:

Notes:

LAUGHING GULL
Leucophaeus atricilla

Date:

Location:

Notes:

FRANKLIN'S GULL
Leucophaeus pipixcan

Date:

Location:

Notes:

HEERMANN'S GULL
Larus heermanni

Date:

Location:

Notes:

MEW GULL *Larus canus*	Date:	Location:
Notes:		

RING-BILLED GULL *Larus delawarensis*	Date:	Location:
Notes:		

WESTERN GULL *Larus occidentalis*	Date:	Location:
Notes:		

YELLOW-FOOTED GULL *Larus livens*	Date:	Location:
Notes:		

CALIFORNIA GULL *Larus californicus*	Date:	Location:
Notes:		

HERRING GULL *Larus argentatus*	Date:	Location:
Notes:		

ICELAND GULL
Larus glaucoides

Date:

Location:

Notes:

LESSER BLACK-BACKED GULL
Larus fuscus

Date:

Location:

Notes:

SLATY-BACKED GULL
Larus schistisagus

Date:

Location:

Notes:

GLAUCOUS-WINGED GULL
Larus glaucescens

Date:

Location:

Notes:

GLAUCOUS GULL
Larus hyperboreus

Date:

Location:

Notes:

GREAT BLACK-BACKED GULL
Larus marinus

Date:

Location:

Notes:

BROWN NODDY *Anous stolidus*	Date:	Location:
Notes:		

BLACK NODDY *Anous minutus*	Date:	Location:
Notes:		

SOOTY TERN *Onychoprion fuscatus*	Date:	Location:
Notes:		

BRIDLED TERN *Onychoprion anaethetus*	Date:	Location:
Notes:		

ALEUTIAN TERN *Onychoprion aleuticus*	Date:	Location:
Notes:		

LEAST TERN *Sternula antillarum*	Date:	Location:
Notes:		

GULL-BILLED TERN *Gelochelidon nilotica*	Date:	Location:
Notes:		

CASPIAN TERN *Hydroprogne caspia*	Date:	Location:
Notes:		

BLACK TERN *Chlidonias niger*	Date:	Location:
Notes:		

ROSEATE TERN *Sterna dougallii*	Date:	Location:
Notes:		

COMMON TERN *Sterna hirundo*	Date:	Location:
Notes:		

ARCTIC TERN *Sterna paradisaea*	Date:	Location:
Notes:		

FORSTER'S TERN *Sterna forsteri*	Date:	Location:
Notes:		

ROYAL TERN *Thalasseus maximus*	Date:	Location:
Notes:		

SANDWICH TERN *Thalasseus sandvicensis*	Date:	Location:
Notes:		

ELEGANT TERN *Thalasseus elegans*	Date:	Location:
Notes:		

BLACK SKIMMER *Rynchops niger*	Date:	Location:
Notes:		

Notes:

WHITE-TAILED TROPICBIRD *Phaethon lepturus*	Date:	Location:
Notes:		

RED-BILLED TROPICBIRD *Phaethon aethereus*	Date:	Location:
Notes:		

RED-TAILED TROPICBIRD *Phaethon rubricauda*	Date:	Location:
Notes:		

RED-THROATED LOON *Gavia stellata*	Date:	Location:
Notes:		

ARCTIC LOON *Gavia arctica*	Date:	Location:
Notes:		

PACIFIC LOON *Gavia pacifica*	Date:	Location:
Notes:		

COMMON LOON *Gavia immer*	Date:	Location:

Notes:

YELLOW-BILLED LOON *Gavia adamsii*	Date:	Location:

Notes:

Notes:

LAYSAN ALBATROSS *Phoebastria immutabilis*	Date:	Location:
Notes:		

BLACK-FOOTED ALBATROSS *Phoebastria nigripes*	Date:	Location:
Notes:		

SHORT-TAILED ALBATROSS *Phoebastria albatrus*	Date:	Location:
Notes:		

WILSON'S STORM-PETREL *Oceanites oceanicus*	Date:	Location:
Notes:		

WHITE-FACED STORM-PETREL *Pelagodroma marina*	Date:	Location:
Notes:		

FORK-TAILED STORM-PETREL *Oceanodroma furcata*	Date:	Location:
Notes:		

LEACH'S STORM-PETREL
Oceanodroma leucorhoa

Date:

Location:

Notes:

TOWNSEND'S STORM-PETREL
Oceanodroma socorroensis

Date:

Location:

Notes:

ASHY STORM-PETREL
Oceanodroma homochroa

Date:

Location:

Notes:

BAND-RUMPED STORM-PETREL
Oceanodroma castro

Date:

Location:

Notes:

BLACK STORM-PETREL
Oceanodroma melania

Date:

Location:

Notes:

TRISTRAM'S STORM-PETREL
Oceanodroma tristrami

Date:

Location:

Notes:

LEAST STORM-PETREL
Oceanodroma microsoma

Date:

Location:

Notes:

NORTHERN FULMAR
Fulmarus glacialis

Date:

Location:

Notes:

TRINDADE PETREL
Pterodroma arminjoniana

Date:

Location:

Notes:

MURPHY'S PETREL
Pterodroma ultima

Date:

Location:

Notes:

FEA'S PETREL
Pterodroma feae

Date:

Location:

Notes:

MOTTLED PETREL
Pterodroma inexpectata

Date:

Location:

Notes:

BERMUDA PETREL
Pterodroma cahow

Date:

Location:

Notes:

BLACK-CAPPED PETREL
Pterodroma hasitata

Date:

Location:

Notes:

JUAN FERNANDEZ PETREL
Pterodroma externa

Date:

Location:

Notes:

HAWAIIAN PETREL
Pterodroma sandwichensis

Date:

Location:

Notes:

COOK'S PETREL
Pterodroma cookii

Date:

Location:

Notes:

BULWER'S PETREL
Bulweria bulwerii

Date:

Location:

Notes:

CORY'S SHEARWATER
Calonectris diomedea

Date:

Location:

Notes:

PINK-FOOTED SHEARWATER
Ardenna creatopus

Date:

Location:

Notes:

FLESH-FOOTED SHEARWATER
Ardenna carneipes

Date:

Location:

Notes:

GREAT SHEARWATER
Ardenna gravis

Date:

Location:

Notes:

WEDGE-TAILED SHEARWATER
Ardenna pacifica

Date:

Location:

Notes:

BULLER'S SHEARWATER
Ardenna bulleri

Date:

Location:

Notes:

SHEARWATERS

SOOTY SHEARWATER *Ardenna grisea*	Date:	Location:
Notes:		

SHORT-TAILED SHEARWATER *Ardenna tenuirostris*	Date:	Location:
Notes:		

MANX SHEARWATER *Puffinus puffinus*	Date:	Location:
Notes:		

NEWELL'S SHEARWATER *Puffinus newelli*	Date:	Location:
Notes:		

BLACK-VENTED SHEARWATER *Puffinus opisthomelas*	Date:	Location:
Notes:		

AUDUBON'S SHEARWATER *Puffinus lherminieri*	Date:	Location:
Notes:		

WOOD STORK
Mycteria americana

Date:

Location:

Notes:

MAGNIFICENT FRIGATEBIRD
Fregata magnificens

Date:

Location:

Notes:

GREAT FRIGATEBIRD
Fregata minor

Date:

Location:

Notes:

MASKED BOOBY
Sula dactylatra

Date:

Location:

Notes:

BROWN BOOBY
Sula leucogaster

Date:

Location:

Notes:

RED-FOOTED BOOBY
Sula sula

Date:

Location:

Notes:

NORTHERN GANNET *Morus bassanus*	Date:	Location:
Notes:		

ANHINGA *Anhinga anhinga*	Date:	Location:
Notes:		

BRANDT'S CORMORANT *Phalacrocorax penicillatus*	Date:	Location:
Notes:		

RED-FACED CORMORANT *Phalacrocorax urile*	Date:	Location:
Notes:		

PELAGIC CORMORANT *Phalacrocorax pelagicus*	Date:	Location:
Notes:		

GREAT CORMORANT *Phalacrocorax carbo*	Date:	Location:
Notes:		

NEOTROPIC CORMORANT
Phalacrocorax brasilianus

Date:

Location:

Notes:

DOUBLE-CRESTED CORMORANT
Phalacrocorax auritus

Date:

Location:

Notes:

AMERICAN WHITE PELICAN
Pelecanus erythrorhynchos

Date:

Location:

Notes:

BROWN PELICAN
Pelecanus occidentalis

Date:

Location:

Notes:

Notes:

AMERICAN BITTERN *Botaurus lentiginosus*	Date:	Location:
Notes:		

LEAST BITTERN *Ixobrychus exilis*	Date:	Location:
Notes:		

GREAT BLUE HERON *Ardea herodias*	Date:	Location:
Notes:		

GREAT EGRET *Ardea alba*	Date:	Location:
Notes:		

SNOWY EGRET *Egretta thula*	Date:	Location:
Notes:		

LITTLE BLUE HERON *Egretta caerulea*	Date:	Location:
Notes:		

TRICOLORED HERON
Egretta tricolor

Date:

Location:

Notes:

REDDISH EGRET
Egretta rufescens

Date:

Location:

Notes:

CATTLE EGRET
Bubulcus ibis

Date:

Location:

Notes:

GREEN HERON
Butorides virescens

Date:

Location:

Notes:

BLACK-CROWNED NIGHT-HERON
Nycticorax nycticorax

Date:

Location:

Notes:

YELLOW-CROWNED NIGHT-HERON
Nyctanassa violacea

Date:

Location:

Notes:

WHITE IBIS *Eudocimus albus*	Date:	Location:
Notes:		

GLOSSY IBIS *Plegadis falcinellus*	Date:	Location:
Notes:		

WHITE-FACED IBIS *Plegadis chihi*	Date:	Location:
Notes:		

ROSEATE SPOONBILL *Platalea ajaja*	Date:	Location:
Notes:		

Notes:

CALIFORNIA CONDOR
Gymnogyps californianus

Date:

Location:

Notes:

BLACK VULTURE
Coragyps atratus

Date:

Location:

Notes:

TURKEY VULTURE
Cathartes aura

Date:

Location:

Notes:

OSPREY
Pandion haliaetus

Date:

Location:

Notes:

WHITE-TAILED KITE
Elanus leucurus

Date:

Location:

Notes:

HOOK-BILLED KITE
Chondrohierax uncinatus

Date:

Location:

Notes:

SWALLOW-TAILED KITE
Elanoides forficatus

Date:

Location:

Notes:

GOLDEN EAGLE
Aquila chrysaetos

Date:

Location:

Notes:

SNAIL KITE
Rostrhamus sociabilis

Date:

Location:

Notes:

MISSISSIPPI KITE
Ictinia mississippiensis

Date:

Location:

Notes:

NORTHERN HARRIER
Circus hudsonius

Date:

Location:

Notes:

SHARP-SHINNED HAWK
Accipiter striatus

Date:

Location:

Notes:

COOPER'S HAWK
Accipiter cooperii

Date:

Location:

Notes:

NORTHERN GOSHAWK
Accipiter gentilis

Date:

Location:

Notes:

BALD EAGLE
Haliaeetus leucocephalus

Date:

Location:

Notes:

COMMON BLACK HAWK
Buteogallus anthracinus

Date:

Location:

Notes:

HARRIS'S HAWK
Parabuteo unicinctus

Date:

Location:

Notes:

WHITE-TAILED HAWK
Geranoaetus albicaudatus

Date:

Location:

Notes:

GRAY HAWK
Buteo plagiatus

Date:

Location:

Notes:

RED-SHOULDERED HAWK
Buteo lineatus

Date:

Location:

Notes:

BROAD-WINGED HAWK
Buteo platypterus

Date:

Location:

Notes:

SHORT-TAILED HAWK
Buteo brachyurus

Date:

Location:

Notes:

SWAINSON'S HAWK
Buteo swainsoni

Date:

Location:

Notes:

ZONE-TAILED HAWK
Buteo albonotatus

Date:

Location:

Notes:

RED-TAILED HAWK *Buteo jamaicensis*	Date:	Location:
Notes:		

ROUGH-LEGGED HAWK *Buteo lagopus*	Date:	Location:
Notes:		

FERRUGINOUS HAWK *Buteo regalis*	Date:	Location:
Notes:		

Notes:

BARN OWL *Tyto alba*	Date:	Location:
Notes:		

FLAMMULATED OWL *Psiloscops flammeolus*	Date:	Location:
Notes:		

WHISKERED SCREECH-OWL *Megascops trichopsis*	Date:	Location:
Notes:		

WESTERN SCREECH-OWL *Megascops kennicottii*	Date:	Location:
Notes:		

EASTERN SCREECH-OWL *Megascops asio*	Date:	Location:
Notes:		

GREAT HORNED OWL *Bubo virginianus*	Date:	Location:
Notes:		

SNOWY OWL *Bubo scandiacus*	Date:	Location:
Notes:		

NORTHERN HAWK OWL *Surnia ulula*	Date:	Location:
Notes:		

NORTHERN PYGMY-OWL *Glaucidium gnoma*	Date:	Location:
Notes:		

FERRUGINOUS PYGMY-OWL *Glaucidium brasilianum*	Date:	Location:
Notes:		

ELF OWL *Micrathene whitneyi*	Date:	Location:
Notes:		

BURROWING OWL *Athene cunicularia*	Date:	Location:
Notes:		

SPOTTED OWL *Strix occidentalis*	Date:	Location:
Notes:		

BARRED OWL *Strix varia*	Date:	Location:
Notes:		

GREAT GRAY OWL *Strix nebulosa*	Date:	Location:
Notes:		

LONG-EARED OWL *Asio otus*	Date:	Location:
Notes:		

SHORT-EARED OWL *Asio flammeus*	Date:	Location:
Notes:		

BOREAL OWL *Aegolius funereus*	Date:	Location:
Notes:		

NORTHERN SAW-WHET OWL *Aegolius acadicus*	Date:	Location:
Notes:		

Notes:

ELEGANT TROGON *Trogon elegans*	Date:	Location:
Notes:		

RINGED KINGFISHER *Megaceryle torquata*	Date:	Location:
Notes:		

BELTED KINGFISHER *Megaceryle alcyon*	Date:	Location:
Notes:		

GREEN KINGFISHER *Chloroceryle americana*	Date:	Location:
Notes:		

WILLIAMSON'S SAPSUCKER *Sphyrapicus thyroideus*	Date:	Location:
Notes:		

YELLOW-BELLIED SAPSUCKER *Sphyrapicus varius*	Date:	Location:
Notes:		

RED-NAPED SAPSUCKER
Sphyrapicus nuchalis

Date:

Location:

Notes:

RED-BREASTED SAPSUCKER
Sphyrapicus ruber

Date:

Location:

Notes:

LEWIS'S WOODPECKER
Melanerpes lewis

Date:

Location:

Notes:

RED-HEADED WOODPECKER
Melanerpes erythrocephalus

Date:

Location:

Notes:

ACORN WOODPECKER
Melanerpes formicivorus

Date:

Location:

Notes:

GILA WOODPECKER
Melanerpes uropygialis

Date:

Location:

Notes:

GOLDEN-FRONTED WOODPECKER *Melanerpes aurifrons*	Date:	Location:
Notes:		

RED-BELLIED WOODPECKER *Melanerpes carolinus*	Date:	Location:
Notes:		

AMERICAN THREE-TOED WOODPECKER *Picoides dorsalis*	Date:	Location:
Notes:		

BLACK-BACKED WOODPECKER *Picoides arcticus*	Date:	Location:
Notes:		

DOWNY WOODPECKER *Dryobates pubescens*	Date:	Location:
Notes:		

NUTTALL'S WOODPECKER *Dryobates nuttallii*	Date:	Location:
Notes:		

CRESTED CARACARA
Caracara cheriway

Date:

Location:

Notes:

AMERICAN KESTREL
Falco sparverius

Date:

Location:

Notes:

MERLIN
Falco columbarius

Date:

Location:

Notes:

APLOMADO FALCON
Falco femoralis

Date:

Location:

Notes:

GYRFALCON
Falco rusticolus

Date:

Location:

Notes:

PEREGRINE FALCON
Falco peregrinus

Date:

Location:

Notes:

PRAIRIE FALCON *Falco mexicanus*	Date:	Location:
Notes:		

Notes:

ROSY-FACED LOVEBIRD (I) *Agapornis roseicollis*	Date:	Location:
Notes:		

MONK PARAKEET (I) *Myiopsitta monachus*	Date:	Location:
Notes:		

WHITE-WINGED PARAKEET (I) *Brotogeris versicolurus*	Date:	Location:
Notes:		

RED-CROWNED PARROT (I) *Amazona viridigenalis*	Date:	Location:
Notes:		

NANDAY PARAKEET (I) *Aratinga nenday*	Date:	Location:
Notes:		

GREEN PARAKEET (I) *Psittacara holochlorus*	Date:	Location:
Notes:		

NORTHERN BEARDLESS-TYRANNULET
Camptostoma imberbe

Date:

Location:

Notes:

OLIVE-SIDED FLYCATCHER
Contopus cooperi

Date:

Location:

Notes:

GREATER PEWEE
Contopus pertinax

Date:

Location:

Notes:

WESTERN WOOD-PEWEE
Contopus sordidulus

Date:

Location:

Notes:

EASTERN WOOD-PEWEE
Contopus virens

Date:

Location:

Notes:

YELLOW-BELLIED FLYCATCHER
Empidonax flaviventris

Date:

Location:

Notes:

ACADIAN FLYCATCHER
Empidonax virescens

Date:

Location:

Notes:

ALDER FLYCATCHER
Empidonax alnorum

Date:

Location:

Notes:

WILLOW FLYCATCHER
Empidonax traillii

Date:

Location:

Notes:

LEAST FLYCATCHER
Empidonax minimus

Date:

Location:

Notes:

HAMMOND'S FLYCATCHER
Empidonax hammondii

Date:

Location:

Notes:

GRAY FLYCATCHER
Empidonax wrightii

Date:

Location:

Notes:

DUSKY FLYCATCHER *Empidonax oberholseri*	Date:	Location:

Notes:

PACIFIC-SLOPE FLYCATCHER *Empidonax difficilis*	Date:	Location:

Notes:

CORDILLERAN FLYCATCHER *Empidonax occidentalis*	Date:	Location:

Notes:

BUFF-BREASTED FLYCATCHER *Empidonax fulvifrons*	Date:	Location:

Notes:

BLACK PHOEBE *Sayornis nigricans*	Date:	Location:

Notes:

EASTERN PHOEBE *Sayornis phoebe*	Date:	Location:

Notes:

SAY'S PHOEBE *Sayornis saya*	Date:	Location:
Notes:		

VERMILION FLYCATCHER *Pyrocephalus rubinus*	Date:	Location:
Notes:		

DUSKY-CAPPED FLYCATCHER *Myiarchus tuberculifer*	Date:	Location:
Notes:		

ASH-THROATED FLYCATCHER *Myiarchus cinerascens*	Date:	Location:
Notes:		

GREAT CRESTED FLYCATCHER *Myiarchus crinitus*	Date:	Location:
Notes:		

BROWN-CRESTED FLYCATCHER *Myiarchus tyrannulus*	Date:	Location:
Notes:		

LA SAGRA'S FLYCATCHER *Myiarchus sagrae*	Date:	Location:
Notes:		

GREAT KISKADEE *Pitangus sulphuratus*	Date:	Location:
Notes:		

SULPHUR-BELLIED FLYCATCHER *Myiodynastes luteiventris*	Date:	Location:
Notes:		

TROPICAL KINGBIRD *Tyrannus melancholicus*	Date:	Location:
Notes:		

COUCH'S KINGBIRD *Tyrannus couchii*	Date:	Location:
Notes:		

CASSIN'S KINGBIRD *Tyrannus vociferans*	Date:	Location:
Notes:		

THICK-BILLED KINGBIRD
Tyrannus crassirostris

Date:

Location:

Notes:

WESTERN KINGBIRD
Tyrannus verticalis

Date:

Location:

Notes:

EASTERN KINGBIRD
Tyrannus tyrannus

Date:

Location:

Notes:

GRAY KINGBIRD
Tyrannus dominicensis

Date:

Location:

Notes:

SCISSOR-TAILED FLYCATCHER
Tyrannus forficatus

Date:

Location:

Notes:

FORK-TAILED FLYCATCHER
Tyrannus savana

Date:

Location:

Notes:

ROSE-THROATED BECARD *Pachyramphus aglaiae*	Date:	Location:
Notes:		

LOGGERHEAD SHRIKE *Lanius ludovicianus*	Date:	Location:
Notes:		

NORTHERN SHRIKE *Lanius borealis*	Date:	Location:
Notes:		

BLACK-CAPPED VIREO *Vireo atricapilla*	Date:	Location:
Notes:		

WHITE-EYED VIREO *Vireo griseus*	Date:	Location:
Notes:		

BELL'S VIREO *Vireo bellii*	Date:	Location:
Notes:		

GRAY VIREO *Vireo vicinior*	Date:	Location:
Notes:		

HUTTON'S VIREO *Vireo huttoni*	Date:	Location:
Notes:		

YELLOW-THROATED VIREO *Vireo flavifrons*	Date:	Location:
Notes:		

CASSIN'S VIREO *Vireo cassinii*	Date:	Location:
Notes:		

BLUE-HEADED VIREO *Vireo solitarius*	Date:	Location:
Notes:		

PLUMBEOUS VIREO *Vireo plumbeus*	Date:	Location:
Notes:		

PHILADELPHIA VIREO
Vireo philadelphicus

Date:

Location:

Notes:

WARBLING VIREO
Vireo gilvus

Date:

Location:

Notes:

RED-EYED VIREO
Vireo olivaceus

Date:

Location:

Notes:

YELLOW-GREEN VIREO
Vireo flavoviridis

Date:

Location:

Notes:

BLACK-WHISKERED VIREO
Vireo altiloquus

Date:

Location:

Notes:

Notes:

CANADA JAY *Perisoreus canadensis*	Date:	Location:
Notes:		

GREEN JAY *Cyanocorax yncas*	Date:	Location:
Notes:		

PINYON JAY *Gymnorhinus cyanocephalus*	Date:	Location:
Notes:		

STELLER'S JAY *Cyanocitta stelleri*	Date:	Location:
Notes:		

BLUE JAY *Cyanocitta cristata*	Date:	Location:
Notes:		

FLORIDA SCRUB-JAY *Aphelocoma coerulescens*	Date:	Location:
Notes:		

ISLAND SCRUB-JAY
Aphelocoma insularis

Date:

Location:

Notes:

CALIFORNIA SCRUB-JAY
Aphelocoma californica

Date:

Location:

Notes:

WOODHOUSE'S SCRUB-JAY
Aphelocoma woodhouseii

Date:

Location:

Notes:

MEXICAN JAY
Aphelocoma wollweberi

Date:

Location:

Notes:

BLACK-BILLED MAGPIE
Pica hudsonia

Date:

Location:

Notes:

YELLOW-BILLED MAGPIE
Pica nuttalli

Date:

Location:

Notes:

CLARK'S NUTCRACKER
Nucifraga columbiana

Date:

Location:

Notes:

AMERICAN CROW
Corvus brachyrhynchos

Date:

Location:

Notes:

NORTHWESTERN CROW
Corvus caurinus

Date:

Location:

Notes:

FISH CROW
Corvus ossifragus

Date:

Location:

Notes:

CHIHUAHUAN RAVEN
Corvus cryptoleucus

Date:

Location:

Notes:

COMMON RAVEN
Corvus corax

Date:

Location:

Notes:

HORNED LARK *Eremophila alpestris*	Date:	Location:
Notes:		

EURASIAN SKYLARK *Alauda arvensis*	Date:	Location:
Notes:		

NORTHERN ROUGH-WINGED SWALLOW *Stelgidopteryx serripennis*	Date:	Location:
Notes:		

PURPLE MARTIN *Progne subis*	Date:	Location:
Notes:		

TREE SWALLOW *Tachycineta bicolor*	Date:	Location:
Notes:		

VIOLET-GREEN SWALLOW *Tachycineta thalassina*	Date:	Location:
Notes:		

BANK SWALLOW
Riparia riparia

Date:

Location:

Notes:

BARN SWALLOW
Hirundo rustica

Date:

Location:

Notes:

CLIFF SWALLOW
Petrochelidon pyrrhonota

Date:

Location:

Notes:

CAVE SWALLOW
Petrochelidon fulva

Date:

Location:

Notes:

CAROLINA CHICKADEE
Poecile carolinensis

Date:

Location:

Notes:

BLACK-CAPPED CHICKADEE
Poecile atricapillus

Date:

Location:

Notes:

MOUNTAIN CHICKADEE
Poecile gambeli

Date:

Location:

Notes:

MEXICAN CHICKADEE
Poecile sclateri

Date:

Location:

Notes:

CHESTNUT-BACKED CHICKADEE
Poecile rufescens

Date:

Location:

Notes:

BOREAL CHICKADEE
Poecile hudsonicus

Date:

Location:

Notes:

GRAY-HEADED CHICKADEE
Poecile cinctus

Date:

Location:

Notes:

BRIDLED TITMOUSE
Baeolophus wollweberi

Date:

Location:

Notes:

OAK TITMOUSE *Baeolophus inornatus*	Date:	Location:
Notes:		

JUNIPER TITMOUSE *Baeolophus ridgwayi*	Date:	Location:
Notes:		

TUFTED TITMOUSE *Baeolophus bicolor*	Date:	Location:
Notes:		

BLACK-CRESTED TITMOUSE *Baeolophus atricristatus*	Date:	Location:
Notes:		

VERDIN *Auriparus flaviceps*	Date:	Location:
Notes:		

BUSHTIT *Psaltriparus minimus*	Date:	Location:
Notes:		

RED-BREASTED NUTHATCH *Sitta canadensis*	Date:	Location:
Notes:		

WHITE-BREASTED NUTHATCH *Sitta carolinensis*	Date:	Location:
Notes:		

PYGMY NUTHATCH *Sitta pygmaea*	Date:	Location:
Notes:		

BROWN-HEADED NUTHATCH *Sitta pusilla*	Date:	Location:
Notes:		

BROWN CREEPER *Certhia americana*	Date:	Location:
Notes:		

ROCK WREN *Salpinctes obsoletus*	Date:	Location:
Notes:		

CANYON WREN	Date:	Location:
Catherpes mexicanus		
Notes:		

HOUSE WREN	Date:	Location:
Troglodytes aedon		
Notes:		

PACIFIC WREN	Date:	Location:
Troglodytes pacificus		
Notes:		

WINTER WREN	Date:	Location:
Troglodytes hiemalis		
Notes:		

SEDGE WREN	Date:	Location:
Cistothorus platensis		
Notes:		

MARSH WREN	Date:	Location:
Cistothorus palustris		
Notes:		

CAROLINA WREN
Thryothorus ludovicianus

Date:

Location:

Notes:

BEWICK'S WREN
Thryomanes bewickii

Date:

Location:

Notes:

CACTUS WREN
Campylorhynchus brunneicapillus

Date:

Location:

Notes:

BLUE-GRAY GNATCATCHER
Polioptila caerulea

Date:

Location:

Notes:

CALIFORNIA GNATCATCHER
Polioptila californica

Date:

Location:

Notes:

BLACK-TAILED GNATCATCHER
Polioptila melanura

Date:

Location:

Notes:

BLACK-CAPPED GNATCATCHER *Polioptila nigriceps*	Date:	Location:
Notes:		

AMERICAN DIPPER *Cinclus mexicanus*	Date:	Location:
Notes:		

RED-WHISKERED BULBUL (I) *Pycnonotus jocosus*	Date:	Location:
Notes:		

GOLDEN CROWNED KINGLET *Regulus satrapa*	Date:	Location:
Notes:		

RUBY-CROWNED KINGLET *Regulus calendula*	Date:	Location:
Notes:		

ARCTIC WARBLER *Phylloscopus borealis*	Date:	Location:
Notes:		

WRENTIT *Chamaea fasciata*	Date:	Location:
Notes:		

BLUETHROAT *Luscinia svecica*	Date:	Location:
Notes:		

SIBERIAN RUBYTHROAT *Calliope calliope*	Date:	Location:
Notes:		

NORTHERN WHEATEAR *Oenanthe oenanthe*	Date:	Location:
Notes:		

Notes:

EASTERN BLUEBIRD *Sialia sialis*	Date:	Location:
Notes:		

WESTERN BLUEBIRD *Sialia mexicana*	Date:	Location:
Notes:		

MOUNTAIN BLUEBIRD *Sialia currucoides*	Date:	Location:
Notes:		

TOWNSEND'S SOLITAIRE *Myadestes townsendi*	Date:	Location:
Notes:		

VARIED THRUSH *Ixoreus naevius*	Date:	Location:
Notes:		

VEERY *Catharus fuscescens*	Date:	Location:
Notes:		

GRAY-CHEEKED THRUSH
Catharus minimus

Date:

Location:

Notes:

BICKNELL'S THRUSH
Catharus bicknelli

Date:

Location:

Notes:

SWAINSON'S THRUSH
Catharus ustulatus

Date:

Location:

Notes:

HERMIT THRUSH
Catharus guttatus

Date:

Location:

Notes:

WOOD THRUSH
Hylocichla mustelina

Date:

Location:

Notes:

CLAY-COLORED THRUSH
Turdus grayi

Date:

Location:

Notes:

AMERICAN ROBIN
Turdus migratorius

Date:

Location:

Notes:

RUFOUS-BACKED ROBIN
Turdus rufopalliatus

Date:

Location:

Notes:

EYEBROWED THRUSH
Turdus obscurus

Date:

Location:

Notes:

GRAY CATBIRD
Dumetella carolinensis

Date:

Location:

Notes:

CURVE-BILLED THRASHER
Toxostoma curvirostre

Date:

Location:

Notes:

BROWN THRASHER
Toxostoma rufum

Date:

Location:

Notes:

LONG-BILLED THRASHER
Toxostoma longirostre

Date:

Location:

Notes:

BENDIRE'S THRASHER
Toxostoma bendirei

Date:

Location:

Notes:

CALIFORNIA THRASHER
Toxostoma redivivum

Date:

Location:

Notes:

LECONTE'S THRASHER
Toxostoma lecontei

Date:

Location:

Notes:

CRISSAL THRASHER
Toxostoma crissale

Date:

Location:

Notes:

SAGE THRASHER
Oreoscoptes montanus

Date:

Location:

Notes:

NORTHERN MOCKINGBIRD *Mimus polyglottos*	Date:	Location:
Notes:		

EUROPEAN STARLING (I) *Sturnus vulgaris*	Date:	Location:
Notes:		

COMMON MYNA (I) *Acridotheres tristis*	Date:	Location:
Notes:		

EASTERN YELLOW WAGTAIL *Motacilla tschutschensis*	Date:	Location:
Notes:		

WHITE WAGTAIL *Motacilla alba*	Date:	Location:
Notes:		

OLIVE-BACKED PIPIT *Anthus hodgsoni*	Date:	Location:
Notes:		

RED-THROATED PIPIT
Anthus cervinus

Date:

Location:

Notes:

AMERICAN PIPIT
Anthus rubescens

Date:

Location:

Notes:

SPRAGUE'S PIPIT
Anthus spragueii

Date:

Location:

Notes:

BOHEMIAN WAXWING
Bombycilla garrulus

Date:

Location:

Notes:

CEDAR WAXWING
Bombycilla cedrorum

Date:

Location:

Notes:

PHAINOPEPLA
Phainopepla nitens

Date:

Location:

Notes:

OLIVE WARBLER *Peucedramus taeniatus*	Date:	Location:
Notes:		

Notes:

BRAMBLING *Fringilla montifringilla*	Date:	Location:
Notes:		

EVENING GROSBEAK *Coccothraustes vespertinus*	Date:	Location:
Notes:		

PINE GROSBEAK *Pinicola enucleator*	Date:	Location:
Notes:		

GRAY-CROWNED ROSY-FINCH *Leucosticte tephrocotis*	Date:	Location:
Notes:		

BLACK ROSY-FINCH *Leucosticte atrata*	Date:	Location:
Notes:		

BROWN-CAPPED ROSY-FINCH *Leucosticte australis*	Date:	Location:
Notes:		

HOUSE FINCH
Haemorhous mexicanus

Date:

Location:

Notes:

PURPLE FINCH
Haemorhous purpureus

Date:

Location:

Notes:

CASSIN'S FINCH
Haemorhous cassinii

Date:

Location:

Notes:

COMMON REDPOLL
Acanthis flammea

Date:

Location:

Notes:

HOARY REDPOLL
Acanthis hornemanni

Date:

Location:

Notes:

RED CROSSBILL
Loxia curvirostra

Date:

Location:

Notes:

CASSIA CROSSBILL
Loxia sinesciuris

Date:

Location:

Notes:

WHITE-WINGED CROSSBILL
Loxia leucoptera

Date:

Location:

Notes:

PINE SISKIN
Spinus pinus

Date:

Location:

Notes:

LESSER GOLDFINCH
Spinus psaltria

Date:

Location:

Notes:

LAWRENCE'S GOLDFINCH
Spinus lawrencei

Date:

Location:

Notes:

AMERICAN GOLDFINCH
Spinus tristis

Date:

Location:

Notes:

LAPLAND LONGSPUR
Calcarius lapponicus

Date:

Location:

Notes:

CHESTNUT-COLLARED LONGSPUR
Calcarius ornatus

Date:

Location:

Notes:

SMITH'S LONGSPUR
Calcarius pictus

Date:

Location:

Notes:

MCCOWN'S LONGSPUR
Rhynchophanes mccownii

Date:

Location:

Notes:

SNOW BUNTING
Plectrophenax nivalis

Date:

Location:

Notes:

MCKAY'S BUNTING
Plectrophenax hyperboreus

Date:

Location:

Notes:

RUSTIC BUNTING *Emberiza rustica*	Date:	Location:

Notes:

Notes:

RUFOUS-WINGED SPARROW *Peucaea carpalis*	Date:	Location:
Notes:		

BOTTERI'S SPARROW *Peucaea botterii*	Date:	Location:
Notes:		

CASSIN'S SPARROW *Peucaea cassinii*	Date:	Location:
Notes:		

BACHMAN'S SPARROW *Peucaea aestivalis*	Date:	Location:
Notes:		

GRASSHOPPER SPARROW *Ammodramus savannarum*	Date:	Location:
Notes:		

OLIVE SPARROW *Arremonops rufivirgatus*	Date:	Location:
Notes:		

CHIPPING SPARROW *Spizella passerina*	Date:	Location:
Notes:		

CLAY-COLORED SPARROW *Spizella pallida*	Date:	Location:
Notes:		

BLACK-CHINNED SPARROW *Spizella atrogularis*	Date:	Location:
Notes:		

FIELD SPARROW *Spizella pusilla*	Date:	Location:
Notes:		

BREWER'S SPARROW *Spizella breweri*	Date:	Location:
Notes:		

BLACK-THROATED SPARROW *Amphispiza bilineata*	Date:	Location:
Notes:		

FIVE-STRIPED SPARROW *Amphispiza quinquestriata*	Date:	Location:
Notes:		

LARK SPARROW *Chondestes grammacus*	Date:	Location:
Notes:		

LARK BUNTING *Calamospiza melanocorys*	Date:	Location:
Notes:		

AMERICAN TREE SPARROW *Spizelloides arborea*	Date:	Location:
Notes:		

FOX SPARROW *Passerella iliaca*	Date:	Location:
Notes:		

DARK-EYED JUNCO *Junco hyemalis*	Date:	Location:
Notes:		

YELLOW-EYED JUNCO *Junco phaeonotus*	Date:	Location:
Notes:		

WHITE-CROWNED SPARROW *Zonotrichia leucophrys*	Date:	Location:
Notes:		

GOLDEN-CROWNED SPARROW *Zonotrichia atricapilla*	Date:	Location:
Notes:		

HARRIS'S SPARROW *Zonotrichia querula*	Date:	Location:
Notes:		

WHITE-THROATED SPARROW *Zonotrichia albicollis*	Date:	Location:
Notes:		

SAGEBRUSH SPARROW *Artemisiospiza nevadensis*	Date:	Location:
Notes:		

BELL'S SPARROW
Artemisiospiza belli

Date:

Location:

Notes:

VESPER SPARROW
Pooecetes gramineus

Date:

Location:

Notes:

LECONTE'S SPARROW
Ammospiza leconteii

Date:

Location:

Notes:

SEASIDE SPARROW
Ammospiza maritima

Date:

Location:

Notes:

NELSON'S SPARROW
Ammospiza nelsoni

Date:

Location:

Notes:

SALTMARSH SPARROW
Ammospiza caudacuta

Date:

Location:

Notes:

SAVANNAH SPARROW
Passerculus sandwichensis

Date:

Location:

Notes:

BAIRD'S SPARROW
Centronyx bairdii

Date:

Location:

Notes:

HENSLOW'S SPARROW
Centronyx henslowii

Date:

Location:

Notes:

SONG SPARROW
Melospiza melodia

Date:

Location:

Notes:

LINCOLN'S SPARROW
Melospiza lincolnii

Date:

Location:

Notes:

SWAMP SPARROW
Melospiza georgiana

Date:

Location:

Notes:

CANYON TOWHEE
Melozone fusca

Date:

Location:

Notes:

ABERT'S TOWHEE
Melozone aberti

Date:

Location:

Notes:

CALIFORNIA TOWHEE
Melozone crissalis

Date:

Location:

Notes:

RUFOUS-CROWNED SPARROW
Aimophila ruficeps

Date:

Location:

Notes:

GREEN-TAILED TOWHEE
Pipilo chlorurus

Date:

Location:

Notes:

SPOTTED TOWHEE
Pipilo maculatus

Date:

Location:

Notes:

EASTERN TOWHEE *Pipilo erythrophthalmus*	Date:	Location:

Notes:

Notes:

WESTERN SPINDALIS *Spindalis zena*	Date:	Location:
Notes:		

YELLOW-BREASTED CHAT *Icteria virens*	Date:	Location:
Notes:		

YELLOW-HEADED BLACKBIRD *Xanthocephalus xanthocephalus*	Date:	Location:
Notes:		

BOBOLINK *Dolichonyx oryzivorus*	Date:	Location:
Notes:		

WESTERN MEADOWLARK *Sturnella neglecta*	Date:	Location:
Notes:		

EASTERN MEADOWLARK *Sturnella magna*	Date:	Location:
Notes:		

ORCHARD ORIOLE *Icterus spurius*	Date:	Location:
Notes:		

HOODED ORIOLE *Icterus cucullatus*	Date:	Location:
Notes:		

BULLOCK'S ORIOLE *Icterus bullockii*	Date:	Location:
Notes:		

SPOT-BREASTED ORIOLE (I) *Icterus pectoralis*	Date:	Location:
Notes:		

ALTAMIRA ORIOLE *Icterus gularis*	Date:	Location:
Notes:		

AUDUBON'S ORIOLE *Icterus graduacauda*	Date:	Location:
Notes:		

BALTIMORE ORIOLE *Icterus galbula*	Date:	Location:
Notes:		

SCOTT'S ORIOLE *Icterus parisorum*	Date:	Location:
Notes:		

RED-WINGED BLACKBIRD *Agelaius phoeniceus*	Date:	Location:
Notes:		

TRICOLORED BLACKBIRD *Agelaius tricolor*	Date:	Location:
Notes:		

SHINY COWBIRD *Molothrus bonariensis*	Date:	Location:
Notes:		

BRONZED COWBIRD *Molothrus aeneus*	Date:	Location:
Notes:		

BROWN-HEADED COWBIRD
Molothrus ater

Date:

Location:

Notes:

RUSTY BLACKBIRD
Euphagus carolinus

Date:

Location:

Notes:

BREWER'S BLACKBIRD
Euphagus cyanocephalus

Date:

Location:

Notes:

COMMON GRACKLE
Quiscalus quiscula

Date:

Location:

Notes:

BOAT-TAILED GRACKLE
Quiscalus major

Date:

Location:

Notes:

GREAT-TAILED GRACKLE
Quiscalus mexicanus

		Date:	Location:
	OVENBIRD *Seiurus aurocapilla*		
Notes:			

		Date:	Location:
	WORM-EATING WARBLER *Helmitheros vermivorum*		
Notes:			

		Date:	Location:
	LOUISIANA WATERTHRUSH *Parkesia motacilla*		
Notes:			

		Date:	Location:
	NORTHERN WATERTHRUSH *Parkesia noveboracensis*		
Notes:			

		Date:	Location:
	GOLDEN-WINGED WARBLER *Vermivora chrysoptera*		
Notes:			

		Date:	Location:
	BLUE-WINGED WARBLER *Vermivora cyanoptera*		
Notes:			

BLACK-AND-WHITE WARBLER
Mniotilta varia

Date:

Location:

Notes:

PROTHONOTARY WARBLER
Protonotaria citrea

Date:

Location:

Notes:

SWAINSON'S WARBLER
Limnothlypis swainsonii

Date:

Location:

Notes:

TENNESSEE WARBLER
Oreothlypis peregrina

Date:

Location:

Notes:

ORANGE-CROWNED WARBLER
Oreothlypis celata

Date:

Location:

Notes:

COLIMA WARBLER
Oreothlypis crissalis

Date:

Location:

Notes:

LUCY'S WARBLER
Oreothlypis luciae

Date:

Location:

Notes:

NASHVILLE WARBLER
Oreothlypis ruficapilla

Date:

Location:

Notes:

VIRGINIA'S WARBLER
Oreothlypis virginiae

Date:

Location:

Notes:

CONNECTICUT WARBLER
Oporornis agilis

Date:

Location:

Notes:

MACGILLIVRAY'S WARBLER
Geothlypis tolmiei

Date:

Location:

Notes:

MOURNING WARBLER
Geothlypis philadelphia

Date:

Location:

Notes:

KENTUCKY WARBLER
Geothlypis formosa

Date:

Location:

Notes:

COMMON YELLOWTHROAT
Geothlypis trichas

Date:

Location:

Notes:

HOODED WARBLER
Setophaga citrina

Date:

Location:

Notes:

AMERICAN REDSTART
Setophaga ruticilla

Date:

Location:

Notes:

KIRTLAND'S WARBLER
Setophaga kirtlandii

Date:

Location:

Notes:

CAPE MAY WARBLER
Setophaga tigrina

Date:

Location:

Notes:

CERULEAN WARBLER
Setophaga cerulea

Date:

Location:

Notes:

NORTHERN PARULA
Setophaga americana

Date:

Location:

Notes:

TROPICAL PARULA
Setophaga pitiayumi

Date:

Location:

Notes:

MAGNOLIA WARBLER
Setophaga magnolia

Date:

Location:

Notes:

BAY-BREASTED WARBLER
Setophaga castanea

Date:

Location:

Notes:

BLACKBURNIAN WARBLER
Setophaga fusca

Date:

Location:

Notes:

YELLOW WARBLER
Setophaga petechia

Date:

Location:

Notes:

CHESTNUT-SIDED WARBLER
Setophaga pensylvanica

Date:

Location:

Notes:

BLACKPOLL WARBLER
Setophaga striata

Date:

Location:

Notes:

BLACK-THROATED BLUE WARBLER
Setophaga caerulescens

Date:

Location:

Notes:

PALM WARBLER
Setophaga palmarum

Date:

Location:

Notes:

PINE WARBLER
Setophaga pinus

Date:

Location:

Notes:

YELLOW-RUMPED WARBLER
Setophaga coronata

Date:

Location:

Notes:

YELLOW-THROATED WARBLER
Setophaga dominica

Date:

Location:

Notes:

PRAIRIE WARBLER
Setophaga discolor

Date:

Location:

Notes:

GRACE'S WARBLER
Setophaga graciae

Date:

Location:

Notes:

BLACK-THROATED GRAY WARBLER
Setophaga nigrescens

Date:

Location:

Notes:

TOWNSEND'S WARBLER
Setophaga townsendi

Date:

Location:

Notes:

HERMIT WARBLER
Setophaga occidentalis

Date:

Location:

Notes:

GOLDEN-CHEEKED WARBLER
Setophaga chrysoparia

Date:

Location:

Notes:

BLACK-THROATED GREEN WARBLER
Setophaga virens

Date:

Location:

Notes:

RUFOUS-CAPPED WARBLER
Basileuterus rufifrons

Date:

Location:

Notes:

CANADA WARBLER
Cardellina canadensis

Date:

Location:

Notes:

WILSON'S WARBLER
Cardellina pusilla

Date:

Location:

Notes:

RED-FACED WARBLER
Cardellina rubrifrons

Date:

Location:

Notes:

PAINTED REDSTART
Myioborus pictus

Date:

Location:

Notes:

Notes:

HEPATIC TANAGER *Piranga flava*	Date:	Location:
Notes:		

SUMMER TANAGER *Piranga rubra*	Date:	Location:
Notes:		

SCARLET TANAGER *Piranga olivacea*	Date:	Location:
Notes:		

WESTERN TANAGER *Piranga ludoviciana*	Date:	Location:
Notes:		

FLAME-COLORED TANAGER *Piranga bidentata*	Date:	Location:
Notes:		

NORTHERN CARDINAL *Cardinalis cardinalis*	Date:	Location:
Notes:		

PYRRHULOXIA *Cardinalis sinuatus*	Date:	Location:
Notes:		

ROSE-BREASTED GROSBEAK *Pheucticus ludovicianus*	Date:	Location:
Notes:		

BLACK-HEADED GROSBEAK *Pheucticus melanocephalus*	Date:	Location:
Notes:		

BLUE GROSBEAK *Passerina caerulea*	Date:	Location:
Notes:		

LAZULI BUNTING *Passerina amoena*	Date:	Location:
Notes:		

INDIGO BUNTING *Passerina cyanea*	Date:	Location:
Notes:		

VARIED BUNTING *Passerina versicolor*	Date:	Location:
Notes:		

PAINTED BUNTING *Passerina ciris*	Date:	Location:
Notes:		

DICKCISSEL *Spiza americana*	Date:	Location:
Notes:		

MORELET'S SEEDEATER *Sporophila morelleti*	Date:	Location:
Notes:		

HOUSE SPARROW (I) *Passer domesticus*	Date:	Location:
Notes:		

EURASIAN TREE SPARROW (I) *Passer montanus*	Date:	Location:
Notes:		

SCALY-BREASTED MUNIA (I) *Lonchura punctulata*	Date:	Location:
Notes:		

Notes:

NORTH AMERICAN ACCIDENTAL SPECIES

SPECIES NAME	DATE	LOCATION
DUCKS, GEESE, WATERFOWL		
GRAYLAG GOOSE *Anser anser*		
LESSER WHITE-FRONTED GOOSE *Anser erythropus*		
PINK-FOOTED GOOSE *Anser brachyrhynchus*		
BARNACLE GOOSE *Branta leucopsis*		
COMMON SHELDUCK *Tadorna tadorna*		
BAIKAL TEAL *Sibirionetta formosa*		
GARGANEY *Spatula querquedula*		
FALCATED DUCK *Mareca falcata*		
EASTERN SPOT-BILLED DUCK *Anas zonorhyncha*		
WHITE-CHEEKED PINTAIL *Anas bahamensis*		
COMMON SCOTER *Melanitta nigra*		
PIGEONS, DOVES		
SCALY-NAPED PIGEON *Patagioenas squamosa*		
EUROPEAN TURTLE-DOVE *Streptopelia turtur*		
ORIENTAL TURTLE-DOVE *Streptopelia orientalis*		
RUDDY QUAIL-DOVE *Geotrygon montana*		
KEY WEST QUAIL-DOVE *Geotrygon chrysia*		
ZENAIDA DOVE *Zenaida aurita*		
CUCKOOS		
ORIENTAL CUCKOO *Cuculus optatus*		
NIGHTJARS		
GRAY NIGHTJAR *Caprimulgus jotaka*		
SWIFTS		
WHITE-COLLARED SWIFT *Streptoprocne zonaris*		
WHITE-THROATED NEEDLETAIL *Hirundapus caudacutus*		
COMMON SWIFT *Apus apus*		
PACIFIC SWIFT *Apus pacificus*		

SPECIES NAME	DATE	LOCATION
ANTILLEAN PALM-SWIFT *Tachornis phoenicobia*		
HUMMINGBIRDS		
GREEN-BREASTED MANGO *Anthracothorax prevostii*		
PLAIN-CAPPED STARTHROAT *Heliomaster constantii*		
AMETHYST-THROATED HUMMINGBIRD *Lampornis amethystinus*		
BAHAMA WOODSTAR *Calliphlox evelynae*		
BUMBLEBEE HUMMINGBIRD *Atthis heloisa*		
CINNAMON HUMMINGBIRD *Amazilia rutila*		
XANTUS'S HUMMINGBIRD *Hylocharis xantusii*		
RAILS, GALLINULES, COOTS		
CORN CRAKE *Crex crex*		
PAINT-BILLED CRAKE *Mustelirallus erythrops*		
SPOTTED RAIL *Pardirallus maculatus*		
RUFOUS-NECKED WOOD-RAIL *Aramides axillaris*		
EURASIAN MOORHEN *Gallinula chloropus*		
EURASIAN COOT *Fulica atra*		
FINFOOTS		
SUNGREBE *Heliornis fulica*		
CRANES		
COMMON CRANE *Grus grus*		
THICK-KNEES		
DOUBLE-STRIPED THICK-KNEE *Burhinus bistriatus*		
STILTS		
BLACK-WINGED STILT *Himantopus himantopus*		
OYSTERCATCHERS, PLOVERS & LAPWINGS		
EURASIAN OYSTERCATCHER *Haematopus ostralegus*		
EUROPEAN GOLDEN-PLOVER *Pluvialis apricaria*		
NORTHERN LAPWING *Vanellus vanellus*		
GREATER SAND-PLOVER *Charadrius leschenaultii*		

SPECIES NAME	DATE	LOCATION
COLLARED PLOVER *Charadrius collaris*		
LITTLE RINGED PLOVER *Charadrius dubius*		
EURASIAN DOTTEREL *Charadrius morinellus*		
JACANAS		
NORTHERN JACANA *Jacana spinosa*		
SANDPIPERS & ALLIES		
LITTLE CURLEW *Numenius minutus*		
FAR EASTERN CURLEW *Numenius madagascariensis*		
SLENDER-BILLED CURLEW *Numenius tenuirostris*		
EURASIAN CURLEW *Numenius arquata*		
GREAT KNOT *Calidris tenuirostris*		
BROAD-BILLED SANDPIPER *Calidris falcinellus*		
SPOON-BILLED SANDPIPER *Calidris pygmea*		
LITTLE STINT *Calidris minuta*		
JACK SNIPE *Lymnocryptes minimus*		
EURASIAN WOODCOCK *Scolopax rusticola*		
SOLITARY SNIPE *Gallinago solitaria*		
PIN-TAILED SNIPE *Gallinago stenura*		
GREEN SANDPIPER *Tringa ochropus*		
SPOTTED REDSHANK *Tringa erythropus*		
MARSH SANDPIPER *Tringa stagnatilis*		
COMMON REDSHANK *Tringa totanus*		
PRATINCOLES		
ORIENTAL PRATINCOLE *Glareola maldivarum*		
GULLS		
SWALLOW-TAILED GULL *Creagrus furcatus*		
GRAY-HOODED GULL *Chroicocephalus cirrocephalus*		
BELCHER'S GULL *Larus belcheri*		
BLACK-TAILED GULL *Larus crassirostris*		

SPECIES NAME	DATE	LOCATION
YELLOW-LEGGED GULL *Larus michahellis*		
KELP GULL *Larus dominicanus*		
TERNS		
LARGE-BILLED TERN *Phaetusa simplex*		
WHITE-WINGED TERN *Chlidonias leucopterus*		
WHISKERED TERN *Chlidonias hybrida*		
ALBATROSSES		
YELLOW-NOSED ALBATROSS *Thalassarche chlororhynchos*		
WHITE-CAPPED ALBATROSS *Thalassarche cauta*		
SALVIN'S ALBATROSS *Thalassarche salvini*		
CHATHAM ALBATROSS *Thalassarche eremita*		
BLACK-BROWED ALBATROSS *Thalassarche melanophris*		
LIGHT-MANTLED ALBATROSS *Phoebetria palpebrata*		
WANDERING ALBATROSS *Diomedea exulans*		
STORM-PETRELS		
BLACK-BELLIED STORM-PETREL *Fregetta tropica*		
EUROPEAN STORM-PETREL *Hydrobates pelagicus*		
RINGED STORM-PETREL *Oceanodroma hornbyi*		
SWINHOE'S STORM-PETREL *Oceanodroma monorhis*		
WEDGE-RUMPED STORM-PETREL *Oceanodroma tethys*		
SHEARWATERS, PETRELS		
GRAY-FACED PETREL *Pterodroma gouldi*		
KERMADEC PETREL *Pterodroma neglecta*		
PROVIDENCE PETREL *Pterodroma solandri*		
ZINO'S PETREL *Pterodroma madeira*		
STEJNEGER'S PETREL *Pterodroma longirostris*		
JOUANIN'S PETREL *Bulweria fallax*		
WHITE-CHINNED PETREL *Procellaria aequinoctialis*		
PARKINSON'S PETREL *Procellaria parkinsoni*		

SPECIES NAME	DATE	LOCATION
STREAKED SHEARWATER *Calonectris leucomelas*		
CAPE VERDE SHEARWATER *Calonectris edwardsii*		
BAROLO SHEARWATER *Puffinus baroli*		
STORKS		
JABIRU *Jabiru mycteria*		
FRIGATEBIRDS		
LESSER FRIGATEBIRD *Fregata ariel*		
BOOBIES		
NAZCA BOOBY *Sula granti*		
BLUE-FOOTED BOOBY *Sula nebouxii*		
HERONS, EGRETS, BITTERNS		
YELLOW BITTERN *Ixobrychus sinensis*		
BARE-THROATED TIGER-HERON *Tigrisoma mexicanum*		
GRAY HERON *Ardea cinerea*		
INTERMEDIATE EGRET *Ardea intermedia*		
CHINESE EGRET *Egretta eulophotes*		
LITTLE EGRET *Egretta garzetta*		
WESTERN REEF-HERON *Egretta gularis*		
CHINESE POND-HERON *Ardeola bacchus*		
IBISES		
SCARLET IBIS *Eudocimus ruber*		
HAWKS, EAGLES, KITES		
DOUBLE-TOOTHED KITE *Harpagus bidentatus*		
BLACK KITE *Milvus migrans*		
WHITE-TAILED EAGLE *Haliaeetus albicilla*		
STELLER'S SEA-EAGLE *Haliaeetus pelagicus*		
CRANE HAWK *Geranospiza caerulescens*		
GREAT BLACK HAWK *Buteogallus urubitinga*		
ROADSIDE HAWK *Rupornis magnirostris*		

NORTH AMERICAN ACCIDENTAL SPECIES

SPECIES NAME	DATE	LOCATION
OWLS		
ORIENTAL SCOPS-OWL *Otus sunia*		
MOTTLED OWL *Ciccaba virgata*		
STYGIAN OWL *Asio stygius*		
NORTHERN BOOBOOK *Ninox japonica*		
TROGONS		
EARED QUETZAL *Euptilotis neoxenus*		
HOOPOES		
EURASIAN HOOPOE *Upupa epops*		
KINGFISHERS		
AMAZON KINGFISHER *Chloroceryle amazona*		
WOODPECKERS		
EURASIAN WRYNECK *Jynx torquilla*		
GREAT SPOTTED WOODPECKER *Dendrocopos major*		
FALCONS		
COLLARED FOREST-FALCON *Micrastur semitorquatus*		
EURASIAN KESTREL *Falco tinnunculus*		
RED-FOOTED FALCON *Falco vespertinus*		
EURASIAN HOBBY *Falco subbuteo*		
PARROTS		
THICK-BILLED PARROT *Rynchopsitta pachyrhyncha* (Extirpated)		
FLYCATCHERS		
GREENISH ELAENIA *Myiopagis viridicata*		
WHITE-CRESTED ELAENIA *Elaenia albiceps*		
TUFTED FLYCATCHER *Mitrephanes phaeocercus*		
CUBAN PEWEE *Contopus caribaeus*		
PINE FLYCATCHER *Empidonax affinis*		
NUTTING'S FLYCATCHER *Myiarchus nuttingi*		
SOCIAL FLYCATCHER *Myiozetetes similis*		

158

SPECIES NAME	DATE	LOCATION
PIRATIC FLYCATCHER *Legatus leucophaius*		
VARIEGATED FLYCATCHER *Empidonomus varius*		
CROWNED SLATY FLYCATCHER *Empidonomus aurantioatrocristatus*		
LOGGERHEAD KINGBIRD *Tyrannus caudifasciatus*		
TITYRAS & ALLIES		
MASKED TITYRA *Tityra semifasciata*		
GRAY-COLLARED BECARD *Pachyramphus major*		
SHRIKES		
RED-BACKED SHRIKE *Lanius collurio*		
BROWN SHRIKE *Lanius cristatus*		
VIREOS		
THICK-BILLED VIREO *Vireo crassirostris*		
CUBAN VIREO *Vireo gundlachii*		
YUCATAN VIREO *Vireo magister*		
JAYS		
BROWN JAY *Psilorhinus morio*		
CROWS		
EURASIAN JACKDAW *Corvus monedula*		
TAMAULIPAS CROW *Corvus imparatus*		
SWALLOWS		
CUBAN MARTIN *Progne cryptoleuca*		
GRAY-BREASTED MARTIN *Progne chalybea*		
SOUTHERN MARTIN *Progne elegans*		
BROWN-CHESTED MARTIN *Progne tapera*		
MANGROVE SWALLOW *Tachycineta albilinea*		
BAHAMA SWALLOW *Tachycineta cyaneoviridis*		
COMMON HOUSE-MARTIN *Delichon urbicum*		
WRENS		
SINALOA WREN *Thryophilus sinaloa*		

SPECIES NAME	DATE	LOCATION
LEAF WARBLERS		
WOOD WARBLER *Phylloscopus sibilatrix*		
YELLOW-BROWED WARBLER *Phylloscopus inornatus*		
PALLAS'S LEAF WARBLER *Phylloscopus proregulus*		
DUSKY WARBLER *Phylloscopus fuscatus*		
WILLOW WARBLER *Phylloscopus trochilus*		
COMMON CHIFFCHAFF *Phylloscopus collybita*		
KAMCHATKA LEAF WARBLER *Phylloscopus examinandus*		
REED WARBLERS & ALLIES		
THICK-BILLED WARBLER *Arundinax aedon*		
SEDGE WARBLER *Acrocephalus schoenobaenus*		
BLYTH'S REED WARBLER *Acrocephalus dumetorum*		
GRASSBIRDS & ALLIES		
MIDDENDORFF'S GRASSHOPPER-WARBLER *Locustella ochotensis*		
LANCEOLATED WARBLER *Locustella lanceolata*		
EURASIAN RIVER WARBLER *Locustella fluviatilis*		
SYLVIID WARBLERS		
LESSER WHITETHROAT *Sylvia curruca*		
OLD WORLD FLYCATCHERS		
GRAY-STREAKED FLYCATCHER *Muscicapa griseisticta*		
DARK-SIDED FLYCATCHER *Muscicapa sibirica*		
ASIAN BROWN FLYCATCHER *Muscicapa dauurica*		
SPOTTED FLYCATCHER *Muscicapa striata*		
EUROPEAN ROBIN *Erithacus rubecula*		
RUFOUS-TAILED ROBIN *Larvivora sibilans*		
SIBERIAN BLUE ROBIN *Larvivora cyane*		
RED-FLANKED BLUETAIL *Tarsiger cyanurus*		
NARCISSUS FLYCATCHER *Ficedula narcissina*		
MUGIMAKI FLYCATCHER *Ficedula mugimaki*		

SPECIES NAME	DATE	LOCATION
TAIGA FLYCATCHER *Ficedula albicilla*		
COMMON REDSTART *Phoenicurus phoenicurus*		
SIBERIAN STONECHAT *Saxicola maurus*		
PIED WHEATEAR *Oenanthe pleschanka*		
THRUSHES & ALLIES		
BROWN-BACKED SOLITAIRE *Myadestes occidentalis*		
ORANGE-BILLED NIGHTINGALE-THRUSH *Catharus aurantiirostris*		
BLACK-HEADED NIGHTINGALE-THRUSH *Catharus mexicanus*		
AZTEC THRUSH *Ridgwayia pinicola*		
MISTLE THRUSH *Turdus viscivorus*		
SONG THRUSH *Turdus philomelos*		
REDWING *Turdus iliacus*		
EURASIAN BLACKBIRD *Turdus merula*		
WHITE-THROATED THRUSH *Turdus assimilis*		
RED-LEGGED THRUSH *Turdus plumbeus*		
FIELDFARE *Turdus pilaris*		
DUSKY THRUSH *Turdus eunomus*		
NAUMANN'S THRUSH *Turdus naumanni*		
MOCKINGBIRDS		
BLUE MOCKINGBIRD *Melanotis caerulescens*		
BAHAMA MOCKINGBIRD *Mimus gundlachii*		
ACCENTORS		
SIBERIAN ACCENTOR *Prunella montanella*		
WAGTAILS, PIPITS		
GRAY WAGTAIL *Motacilla cinerea*		
CITRINE WAGTAIL *Motacilla citreola*		
TREE PIPIT *Anthus trivialis*		
PECHORA PIPIT *Anthus gustavi*		

SPECIES NAME	DATE	LOCATION
SILKY-FLYCATCHERS		
GRAY SILKY-FLYCATCHER *Ptiliogonys cinereus*		
FINCHES & ALLIES		
COMMON CHAFFINCH *Fringilla coelebs*		
HAWFINCH *Coccothraustes coccothraustes*		
COMMON ROSEFINCH *Carpodacus erythrinus*		
PALLAS'S ROSEFINCH *Carpodacus roseus*		
EURASIAN BULLFINCH *Pyrrhula pyrrhula*		
ASIAN ROSY-FINCH *Leucosticte arctoa*		
ORIENTAL GREENFINCH *Chloris sinica*		
EURASIAN SISKIN *Spinus spinus*		
OLD WORLD BUNTINGS		
PINE BUNTING *Emberiza leucocephalos*		
YELLOW-THROATED BUNTING *Emberiza elegans*		
PALLAS'S BUNTING *Emberiza pallasi*		
REED BUNTING *Emberiza schoeniclus*		
YELLOW-BREASTED BUNTING *Emberiza aureola*		
LITTLE BUNTING *Emberiza pusilla*		
YELLOW-BROWED BUNTING *Emberiza chrysophrys*		
GRAY BUNTING *Emberiza variabilis*		
NEW WORLD SPARROWS		
WORTHEN'S SPARROW *Spizella wortheni*		
TROUPIALS & ALLIES		
BLACK-VENTED ORIOLE *Icterus wagleri*		
STREAK-BACKED ORIOLE *Icterus pustulatus*		
BLACK-BACKED ORIOLE *Icterus abeillei*		
TAWNY-SHOULDERED BLACKBIRD *Agelaius humeralis*		
NEW WORLD WARBLERS		
CRESCENT-CHESTED WARBLER *Oreothlypis superciliosa*		

SPECIES NAME	DATE	LOCATION
GRAY-CROWNED YELLOWTHROAT *Geothlypis poliocephala*		
FAN-TAILED WARBLER *Basileuterus lachrymosus*		
GOLDEN-CROWNED WARBLER *Basileuterus culicivorus*		
SLATE-THROATED REDSTART *Myioborus miniatus*		
CARDINALS & ALLIES		
CRIMSON-COLLARED GROSBEAK *Rhodothraupis celaeno*		
YELLOW GROSBEAK *Pheucticus chrysopeplus*		
BLUE BUNTING *Cyanocompsa parellina*		
TANAGERS & ALLIES		
RED-LEGGED HONEYCREEPER *Cyanerpes cyaneus*		
BANANAQUIT *Coereba flaveola*		
YELLOW-FACED GRASSQUIT *Tiaris olivaceus*		
BLACK-FACED GRASSQUIT *Tiaris bicolor*		

Great Blue Heron

HAWAIIAN GOOSE
Branta sandvicensis

Date:

Location:

Notes:

LAYSAN DUCK
Anas laysanensis

Date:

Location:

Notes:

HAWAIIAN DUCK
Anas wyvilliana

Date:

Location:

Notes:

INDIAN PEAFOWL (I)
Pavo cristatus

Date:

Location:

Notes:

ERCKEL'S FRANCOLIN (I)
Pternistis erckelii

Date:

Location:

Notes:

BLACK FRANCOLIN (I)
Francolinus francolinus

Date:

Location:

Notes:

GRAY FRANCOLIN (I)
Francolinus pondicerianus

Date:

Location:

Notes:

RED JUNGLEFOWL (I)
Gallus gallus

Date:

Location:

Notes:

KALIJ PHEASANT (I)
Lophura leucomelanos

Date:

Location:

Notes:

ZEBRA DOVE (I)
Geopelia striata

Date:

Location:

Notes:

CHESTNUT-BELLIED SANDGROUSE (I)
Pterocles exustus

Date:

Location:

Notes:

MARIANA SWIFTLET (I)
Aerodramus bartschi

Date:

Location:

Notes:

HAWAIIAN COOT
Fulica alai

Date:

Location:

Notes:

BLUE-GRAY NODDY
Anous ceruleus

Date:

Location:

Notes:

WHITE TERN (I)
Gygis alba

Date:

Location:

Notes:

GRAY-BACKED TERN
Onychoprion lunatus

Date:

Location:

Notes:

WHITE-NECKED PETREL
Pterodroma cervicalis

Date:

Location:

Notes:

BONIN PETREL
Pterodroma hypoleuca

Date:

Location:

Notes:

BLACK-WINGED PETREL *Pterodroma nigripennis*	Date:	Location:
Notes:		

CHRISTMAS SHEARWATER *Puffinus nativitatis*	Date:	Location:
Notes:		

HAWAIIAN HAWK *Buteo solitarius*	Date:	Location:
Notes:		

ROSE-RINGED PARAKEET (I) *Psittacula krameri*	Date:	Location:
Notes:		

HAWAII ELEPAIO *Chasiempis sandwichensis*	Date:	Location:
Notes:		

KAUAI ELEPAIO *Chasiempis sclateri*	Date:	Location:
Notes:		

OAHU ELEPAIO *Chasiempis ibidis*	Date:	Location:

Notes:

HAWAIIAN CROW *Corvus hawaiiensis*	Date:	Location:

Notes:
Recently reintroduced into native Hawaiian forest.

RED-VENTED BULBUL (I) *Pycnonotus cafer*	Date:	Location:

Notes:

JAPANESE BUSH WARBLER (I) *Horornis diphone*	Date:	Location:

Notes:

MILLERBIRD *Acrocephalus familiaris*	Date:	Location:

Notes:

JAPANESE WHITE-EYE (I) *Zosterops japonicus*	Date:	Location:

Notes:

CHINESE HWAMEI (I) *Garrulax canorus*	Date:	Location:
Notes:		

GREATER NECKLACED LAUGHINGTHRUSH (I) *Ianthocincla pectoralis*	Date:	Location:
Notes:		

RED-BILLED LEIOTHRIX (I) *Leiothrix lutea*	Date:	Location:
Notes:		

WHITE-RUMPED SHAMA *Copsychus malabaricus*	Date:	Location:
Notes:		

OMAO *Myadestes obscurus*	Date:	Location:
Notes:		

PUAIOHI *Myadestes palmeri*	Date:	Location:
Notes:		

AKIKIKI
Oreomystis bairdi

Date:

Location:

Notes:

MAUI ALAUAHIO
Paroreomyza montana

Date:

Location:

Notes:

PALILA
Loxioides bailleui

Date:

Location:

Notes:

LAYSAN FINCH
Telespiza cantans

Date:

Location:

Notes:

NIHOA FINCH
Telespiza ultima

Date:

Location:

Notes:

AKOHEKOHE
Palmeria dolei

Date:

Location:

Notes:

APAPANE *Himatione sanguinea*	Date:	Location:
Notes:		

IIWI *Drepanis coccinea*	Date:	Location:
Notes:		

MAUI PARROTBILL *Pseudonestor xanthophrys*	Date:	Location:
Notes:		

AKIAPOLAAU *Hemignathus wilsoni*	Date:	Location:
Notes:		

ANIANIAU *Magumma parva*	Date:	Location:
Notes:		

HAWAII AMAKIHI *Chlorodrepanis virens*	Date:	Location:
Notes:		

OAHU AMAKIHI
Chlorodrepanis flava

Date:

Location:

Notes:

KAUAI AMAKIHI
Chlorodrepanis stejnegeri

Date:

Location:

Notes:

HAWAII CREEPER
Loxops mana

Date:

Location:

Notes:

AKEKEE
Loxops caeruleirostris

Date:

Location:

Notes:

HAWAII AKEPA
Loxops coccineus

Date:

Location:

Notes:

YELLOW-FRONTED CANARY (I)
Crithagra mozambica

Date:

Location:

Notes:

ISLAND CANARY (I) *Serinus canaria*	Date:	Location:
Notes:		

RED-CRESTED CARDINAL (I) *Paroaria coronata*	Date:	Location:
Notes:		

YELLOW-BILLED CARDINAL (I) *Paroaria capitata*	Date:	Location:
Notes:		

SAFFRON FINCH (I) *Sicalis flaveola*	Date:	Location:
Notes:		

YELLOW-FACED GRASSQUIT (I) *Tiaris olivaceus*	Date:	Location:
Notes:		

COMMON WAXBILL (I) *Estrilda astrild*	Date:	Location:
Notes:		

RED AVADAVAT (I)
Amandava amandava

Date:

Location:

Notes:

AFRICAN SILVERBILL (I)
Euodice cantans

Date:

Location:

Notes:

CHESTNUT MUNIA (I)
Lonchura atricapilla

Date:

Location:

Notes:

JAVA SPARROW (I)
Lonchura oryzivora

Date:

Location:

Notes:

Notes:

HAWAIIAN ACCIDENTAL SPECIES

SPECIES NAME	DATE	LOCATION
LITTLE TERN *Sternula albifrons*		
GREAT CRESTED TERN *Thalasseus bergii*		
HERALD PETREL *Pterodroma heraldica*		
TAHITI PETREL *Pseudobulweria rostrata*		
BRYAN'S SHEARWATER *Puffinus bryani*		
CHINESE SPARROWHAWK *Accipiter soloensis*		

EXTINCT SPECIES

The birds listed here are species known to be extinct and species whose status is uncertain and may already be extinct, or on the verge of extinction. Although extinct species will never be seen again, they are deserving of a place in a checklist of birds. They were once part of our landscape, and some, like the Passenger Pigeon, were so numerous it is still shocking that they are gone. Including this list reminds us that we should do more than just look at birds. We should consider ourselves caretakers of the habitats they live in and do all we can to protect birds and the places where they thrive. Additionally, as a keen observer and record-keeper, you can join citizen-science projects such as eBird, Project FeederWatch, and NestWatch. Your contributions will provide valuable data needed to detect changes in bird populations and gauge where conservation is succeeding and where birds need our help to prevent future extinctions.

EXTINCT SPECIES, NORTH AMERICA NORTH OF MEXICO

LABRADOR DUCK *Camptorhynchus labradorius*
PASSENGER PIGEON *Ectopistes migratorius*
ESKIMO CURLEW *Numenius borealis*
GREAT AUK *Pinguinus impennis*
IVORY-BILLED WOODPECKER *Campephilus principalis* **Possibly extinct.**
CAROLINA PARAKEET *Conuropsis carolinensis*
BACHMAN'S WARBLER *Vermivora bachmanii*

EXTINCT SPECIES, HAWAII

LAYSAN RAIL *Zapornia palmeri*
HAWAIIAN RAIL *Zapornia sandwichensis*
KAMAO *Myadestes myadestinus*
AMAUI *Myadestes woahensis*
OLOMAO *Myadestes lanaiensis*
KAUAI OO *Moho braccatus*
OAHU OO *Moho apicalis*

BISHOP'S OO *Moho bishopi*
HAWAII OO *Moho nobilis*
KIOEA *Chaetoptila angustipluma*
POO-ULI *Melamprosops phaeosoma* **Possibly extinct, last seen in 2004.**
OAHU ALAUAHIO *Paroreomyza maculata*
KAKAWAHIE *Paroreomyza flammea*
KONA GROSBEAK *Chloridops kona*
LESSER KOA-FINCH *Rhodacanthis flaviceps*
GREATER KOA-FINCH *Rhodacanthis palmeri*
ULA-AI-HAWANE *Ciridops anna*
LAYSAN HONEYCREEPER *Himatione fraithii*
HAWAII MAMO *Drepanis pacifica*
BLACK MAMO *Drepanis funerea*
OU *Psittirostra psittacea*
LANAI HOOKBILL *Dysmorodrepanis munroi*
KAUAI NUKUPUU *Hemignathus hanapepe*
OAHU NUKUPUU *Hemignathus lucidus*
MAUI NUKUPUU *Hemignathus affinis*
LESSER AKIALOA *Akialoa obscura*
OAHU AKIALOA *Akialoa ellisiana*
KAUAI AKIALOA *Akialoa stejnegeri*
MAUI-NUI AKIALOA *Akialoa lanaiensis*
GREATER AMAKIHI *Viridonia sagittirostris*
OAHU AKEPA *Loxops wolstenholmei*
MAUI AKEPA *Loxops ochraceus*

American
Robins

CHECKLIST
(I) INTRODUCED   (A) ACCIDENTAL   (H) HAWAIIAN

ANSERIFORMES

BLACK-BELLIED WHISTLING-DUCK *Dendrocygna autumnalis*						
FULVOUS WHISTLING-DUCK *Dendrocygna bicolor*						
EMPEROR GOOSE *Anser canagicus*						
SNOW GOOSE *Anser caerulescens*						
ROSS'S GOOSE *Anser rossii*						
GRAYLAG GOOSE *Anser anser* (A)						
GREATER WHITE-FRONTED GOOSE *Anser albifrons*						
LESSER WHITE-FRONTED GOOSE *Anser erythropus* (A)						
TAIGA BEAN-GOOSE *Anser fabalis*						
TUNDRA BEAN-GOOSE *Anser serrirostris*						
PINK-FOOTED GOOSE *Anser brachyrhynchus* (A)						
BRANT *Branta bernicla*						
BARNACLE GOOSE *Branta leucopsis* (A)						
CACKLING GOOSE *Branta hutchinsii*						
CANADA GOOSE *Branta canadensis*						
HAWAIIAN GOOSE *Branta sandvicensis* (H)						
MUTE SWAN *Cygnus olor* (I)						
TRUMPETER SWAN *Cygnus buccinator*						
TUNDRA SWAN *Cygnus columbianus*						
WHOOPER SWAN *Cygnus cygnus*						
EGYPTIAN GOOSE *Alopochen aegyptiaca* (I)						
COMMON SHELDUCK *Tadorna tadorna* (A)						
MUSCOVY DUCK *Cairina moschata*						
WOOD DUCK *Aix sponsa*						
BAIKAL TEAL *Sibirionetta formosa* (A)						
GARGANEY *Spatula querquedula* (A)						
BLUE-WINGED TEAL *Spatula discors*						
CINNAMON TEAL *Spatula cyanoptera*						
NORTHERN SHOVELER *Spatula clypeata*						

GADWALL *Mareca strepera*							
FALCATED DUCK *Mareca falcata* (A)							
EURASIAN WIGEON *Mareca penelope*							
AMERICAN WIGEON *Mareca americana*							
LAYSAN DUCK *Anas laysanensis* (H)							
HAWAIIAN DUCK *Anas wyvilliana* (H)							
EASTERN SPOT-BILLED DUCK *Anas zonorhyncha* (A)							
MALLARD *Anas platyrhynchos*							
MEXICAN DUCK *Anas diazi*							
AMERICAN BLACK DUCK *Anas rubripes*							
MOTTLED DUCK *Anas fulvigula*							
WHITE-CHEEKED PINTAIL *Anas bahamensis* (A)							
NORTHERN PINTAIL *Anas acuta*							
GREEN-WINGED TEAL *Anas crecca*							
CANVASBACK *Aythya valisineria*							
REDHEAD *Aythya americana*							
COMMON POCHARD *Aythya ferina*							
RING-NECKED DUCK *Aythya collaris*							
TUFTED DUCK *Aythya fuligula*							
GREATER SCAUP *Aythya marila*							
LESSER SCAUP *Aythya affinis*							
STELLER'S EIDER *Polysticta stelleri*							
SPECTACLED EIDER *Somateria fischeri*							
KING EIDER *Somateria spectabilis*							
COMMON EIDER *Somateria mollissima*							
HARLEQUIN DUCK *Histrionicus histrionicus*							
SURF SCOTER *Melanitta perspicillata*							
WHITE-WINGED SCOTER *Melanitta deglandi*							
COMMON SCOTER *Melanitta nigra* (A)							
BLACK SCOTER *Melanitta americana*							

Species								
LONG-TAILED DUCK *Clangula hyemalis*								
BUFFLEHEAD *Bucephala albeola*								
COMMON GOLDENEYE *Bucephala clangula*								
BARROW'S GOLDENEYE *Bucephala islandica*								
SMEW *Mergellus albellus*								
HOODED MERGANSER *Lophodytes cucullatus*								
COMMON MERGANSER *Mergus merganser*								
RED-BREASTED MERGANSER *Mergus serrator*								
MASKED DUCK *Nomonyx dominicus*								
RUDDY DUCK *Oxyura jamaicensis*								

GALLIFORMES

Species								
PLAIN CHACHALACA *Ortalis vetula*								
MOUNTAIN QUAIL *Oreortyx pictus*								
NORTHERN BOBWHITE *Colinus virginianus*								
SCALED QUAIL *Callipepla squamata*								
CALIFORNIA QUAIL *Callipepla californica*								
GAMBEL'S QUAIL *Callipepla gambelii*								
MONTEZUMA QUAIL *Cyrtonyx montezumae*								
INDIAN PEAFOWL *Pavo cristatus* (H, I)								
CHUKAR *Alectoris chukar* (I)								
HIMALAYAN SNOWCOCK *Tetraogallus himalayensis* (I)								
ERCKEL'S FRANCOLIN *Pternistis erckelii* (H, I)								
BLACK FRANCOLIN *Francolinus francolinus* (H, I)								
GRAY FRANCOLIN *Francolinus pondicerianus* (H, I)								
RED JUNGLEFOWL *Gallus gallus* (H, I)								
RING-NECKED PHEASANT *Phasianus colchicus* (I)								
KALIJ PHEASANT *Lophura leucomelanos* (H, I)								
GRAY PARTRIDGE *Perdix perdix* (I)								
RUFFED GROUSE *Bonasa umbellus*								
GREATER SAGE-GROUSE *Centrocercus urophasianus*								

GUNNISON SAGE-GROUSE *Centrocercus minimus*							
SPRUCE GROUSE *Falcipennis canadensis*							
WILLOW PTARMIGAN *Lagopus lagopus*							
ROCK PTARMIGAN *Lagopus muta*							
WHITE-TAILED PTARMIGAN *Lagopus leucura*							
DUSKY GROUSE *Dendragapus obscurus*							
SOOTY GROUSE *Dendragapus fuliginosus*							
SHARP-TAILED GROUSE *Tympanuchus phasianellus*							
GREATER PRAIRIE-CHICKEN *Tympanuchus cupido*							
LESSER PRAIRIE-CHICKEN *Tympanuchus pallidicinctus*							
WILD TURKEY *Meleagris gallopavo*							
PHOENICOPTERIFORMES							
AMERICAN FLAMINGO *Phoenicopterus ruber*							
PODICIPEDIFORMES							
LEAST GREBE *Tachybaptus dominicus*							
PIED-BILLED GREBE *Podilymbus podiceps*							
HORNED GREBE *Podiceps auritus*							
RED-NECKED GREBE *Podiceps grisegena*							
EARED GREBE *Podiceps nigricollis*							
WESTERN GREBE *Aechmophorus occidentalis*							
CLARK'S GREBE *Aechmophorus clarkii*							
COLUMBIFORMES							
ROCK PIGEON *Columba livia* (I)							
SCALY-NAPED PIGEON *Patagioenas squamosa* (A)							
WHITE-CROWNED PIGEON *Patagioenas leucocephala*							
RED-BILLED PIGEON *Patagioenas flavirostris*							
BAND-TAILED PIGEON *Patagioenas fasciata*							
EUROPEAN TURTLE-DOVE *Streptopelia turtur* (A)							
ORIENTAL TURTLE-DOVE *Streptopelia orientalis* (A)							
EURASIAN COLLARED-DOVE *Streptopelia decaocto* (I)							

CHECKLIST
(I) INTRODUCED   (A) ACCIDENTAL   (H) HAWAIIAN

SPOTTED DOVE *Streptopelia chinensis* (I)								
ZEBRA DOVE *Geopelia striata* (H, I)								
INCA DOVE *Columbina inca*								
COMMON GROUND-DOVE *Columbina passerina*								
RUDDY GROUND-DOVE *Columbina talpacoti*								
RUDDY QUAIL-DOVE *Geotrygon montana* (A)								
KEY WEST QUAIL-DOVE *Geotrygon chrysia* (A)								
WHITE-TIPPED DOVE *Leptotila verreauxi*								
WHITE-WINGED DOVE *Zenaida asiatica*								
ZENAIDA DOVE *Zenaida aurita* (A)								
MOURNING DOVE *Zenaida macroura*								
PTEROCLIFORMES								
CHESTNUT-BELLIED SANDGROUSE *Pterocles exustus* (H, I)								
CUCULIFORMES								
SMOOTH-BILLED ANI *Crotophaga ani*								
GROOVE-BILLED ANI *Crotophaga sulcirostris*								
GREATER ROADRUNNER *Geococcyx californianus*								
YELLOW-BILLED CUCKOO *Coccyzus americanus*								
MANGROVE CUCKOO *Coccyzus minor*								
BLACK-BILLED CUCKOO *Coccyzus erythropthalmus*								
COMMON CUCKOO *Cuculus canorus*								
ORIENTAL CUCKOO *Cuculus optatus* (A)								
CAPRIMULGIFORMES								
LESSER NIGHTHAWK *Chordeiles acutipennis*								
COMMON NIGHTHAWK *Chordeiles minor*								
ANTILLEAN NIGHTHAWK *Chordeiles gundlachii*								
COMMON PAURAQUE *Nyctidromus albicollis*								
COMMON POORWILL *Phalaenoptilus nuttallii*								
CHUCK-WILL'S-WIDOW *Antrostomus carolinensis*								
BUFF-COLLARED NIGHTJAR *Antrostomus ridgwayi*								

EASTERN WHIP-POOR-WILL *Antrostomus vociferus*								
MEXICAN WHIP-POOR-WILL *Antrostomus arizonae*								
GRAY NIGHTJAR *Caprimulgus jotaka* (A)								
BLACK SWIFT *Cypseloides niger*								
WHITE-COLLARED SWIFT *Streptoprocne zonaris* (A)								
CHIMNEY SWIFT *Chaetura pelagica*								
VAUX'S SWIFT *Chaetura vauxi*								
WHITE-THROATED NEEDLETAIL *Hirundapus caudacutus* (A)								
MARIANA SWIFTLET *Aerodramus bartschi* (H, I)								
COMMON SWIFT *Apus apus* (A)								
PACIFIC SWIFT *Apus pacificus* (A)								
WHITE-THROATED SWIFT *Aeronautes saxatalis*								
ANTILLEAN PALM-SWIFT *Tachornis phoenicobia* (A)								
MEXICAN VIOLETEAR *Colibri thalassinus*								
GREEN-BREASTED MANGO *Anthracothorax prevostii* (A)								
RIVOLI'S HUMMINGBIRD *Eugenes fulgens*								
PLAIN-CAPPED STARTHROAT *Heliomaster constantii* (A)								
AMETHYST-THROATED HUMMINGBIRD *Lampornis amethystinus* (A)								
BLUE-THROATED HUMMINGBIRD *Lampornis clemenciae*								
LUCIFER HUMMINGBIRD *Calothorax lucifer*								
BAHAMA WOODSTAR *Calliphlox evelynae* (A)								
RUBY-THROATED HUMMINGBIRD *Archilochus colubris*								
BLACK-CHINNED HUMMINGBIRD *Archilochus alexandri*								
ANNA'S HUMMINGBIRD *Calypte anna*								
COSTA'S HUMMINGBIRD *Calypte costae*								
BUMBLEBEE HUMMINGBIRD *Atthis heloisa* (A)								
BROAD-TAILED HUMMINGBIRD *Selasphorus platycercus*								
RUFOUS HUMMINGBIRD *Selasphorus rufus*								
ALLEN'S HUMMINGBIRD *Selasphorus sasin*								
CALLIOPE HUMMINGBIRD *Selasphorus calliope*								

BROAD-BILLED HUMMINGBIRD *Cynanthus latirostris*							
BERYLLINE HUMMINGBIRD *Amazilia beryllina*							
BUFF-BELLIED HUMMINGBIRD *Amazilia yucatanensis*							
CINNAMON HUMMINGBIRD *Amazilia rutila* (A)							
VIOLET-CROWNED HUMMINGBIRD *Amazilia violiceps*							
WHITE-EARED HUMMINGBIRD *Hylocharis leucotis*							
XANTUS'S HUMMINGBIRD *Hylocharis xantusii* (A)							
GRUIFORMES							
RIDGWAY'S RAIL *Rallus obsoletus*							
KING RAIL *Rallus elegans*							
CLAPPER RAIL *Rallus crepitans*							
VIRGINIA RAIL *Rallus limicola*							
CORN CRAKE *Crex crex* (A)							
PAINT-BILLED CRAKE *Mustelirallus erythrops* (A)							
SPOTTED RAIL *Pardirallus maculatus* (A)							
RUFOUS-NECKED WOOD-RAIL *Aramides axillaris* (A)							
SORA *Porzana carolina*							
EURASIAN MOORHEN *Gallinula chloropus* (A)							
COMMON GALLINULE *Gallinula galeata*							
EURASIAN COOT *Fulica atra* (A)							
HAWAIIAN COOT *Fulica alai* (H)							
AMERICAN COOT *Fulica americana*							
PURPLE GALLINULE *Porphyrio martinica*							
GRAY-HEADED SWAMPHEN *Porphyrio poliocephalus*							
YELLOW RAIL *Coturnicops noveboracensis*							
BLACK RAIL *Laterallus jamaicensis*							
SUNGREBE *Heliornis fulica* (A)							
LIMPKIN *Aramus guarauna*							
SANDHILL CRANE *Antigone canadensis*							
COMMON CRANE *Grus grus* (A)							

WHOOPING CRANE *Grus americana*								
CHARADRIIFORMES								
DOUBLE-STRIPED THICK-KNEE *Burhinus bistriatus* (A)								
BLACK-WINGED STILT *Himantopus himantopus* (A)								
BLACK-NECKED STILT *Himantopus mexicanus*								
AMERICAN AVOCET *Recurvirostra americana*								
EURASIAN OYSTERCATCHER *Haematopus ostralegus* (A)								
AMERICAN OYSTERCATCHER *Haematopus palliatus*								
BLACK OYSTERCATCHER *Haematopus bachmani*								
BLACK-BELLIED PLOVER *Pluvialis squatarola*								
EUROPEAN GOLDEN-PLOVER *Pluvialis apricaria* (A)								
AMERICAN GOLDEN-PLOVER *Pluvialis dominica*								
PACIFIC GOLDEN-PLOVER *Pluvialis fulva*								
NORTHERN LAPWING *Vanellus vanellus* (A)								
LESSER SAND-PLOVER *Charadrius mongolus*								
GREATER SAND-PLOVER *Charadrius leschenaultii* (A)								
COLLARED PLOVER *Charadrius collaris* (A)								
SNOWY PLOVER *Charadrius nivosus*								
WILSON'S PLOVER *Charadrius wilsonia*								
COMMON RINGED PLOVER *Charadrius hiaticula*								
SEMIPALMATED PLOVER *Charadrius semipalmatus*								
PIPING PLOVER *Charadrius melodus*								
LITTLE RINGED PLOVER *Charadrius dubius* (A)								
KILLDEER *Charadrius vociferus*								
MOUNTAIN PLOVER *Charadrius montanus*								
EURASIAN DOTTEREL *Charadrius morinellus* (A)								
NORTHERN JACANA *Jacana spinosa* (A)								
UPLAND SANDPIPER *Bartramia longicauda*								
BRISTLE-THIGHED CURLEW *Numenius tahitiensis*								
WHIMBREL *Numenius phaeopus*								

LITTLE CURLEW *Numenius minutus* (A)							
LONG-BILLED CURLEW *Numenius americanus*							
FAR EASTERN CURLEW *Numenius madagascariensis* (A)							
SLENDER-BILLED CURLEW *Numenius tenuirostris* (A)							
EURASIAN CURLEW *Numenius arquata* (A)							
BAR-TAILED GODWIT *Limosa lapponica*							
BLACK-TAILED GODWIT *Limosa limosa*							
HUDSONIAN GODWIT *Limosa haemastica*							
MARBLED GODWIT *Limosa fedoa*							
RUDDY TURNSTONE *Arenaria interpres*							
BLACK TURNSTONE *Arenaria melanocephala*							
GREAT KNOT *Calidris tenuirostris* (A)							
RED KNOT *Calidris canutus*							
SURFBIRD *Calidris virgata*							
RUFF *Calidris pugnax*							
BROAD-BILLED SANDPIPER *Calidris falcinellus* (A)							
SHARP-TAILED SANDPIPER *Calidris acuminata*							
STILT SANDPIPER *Calidris himantopus*							
CURLEW SANDPIPER *Calidris ferruginea*							
TEMMINCK'S STINT *Calidris temminckii*							
LONG-TOED STINT *Calidris subminuta*							
SPOON-BILLED SANDPIPER *Calidris pygmea* (A)							
RED-NECKED STINT *Calidris ruficollis*							
SANDERLING *Calidris alba*							
DUNLIN *Calidris alpina*							
ROCK SANDPIPER *Calidris ptilocnemis*							
PURPLE SANDPIPER *Calidris maritima*							
BAIRD'S SANDPIPER *Calidris bairdii*							
LITTLE STINT *Calidris minuta* (A)							
LEAST SANDPIPER *Calidris minutilla*							

(I) INTRODUCED   (A) ACCIDENTAL   (H) HAWAIIAN

WHITE-RUMPED SANDPIPER *Calidris fuscicollis*						
BUFF-BREASTED SANDPIPER *Calidris subruficollis*						
PECTORAL SANDPIPER *Calidris melanotos*						
SEMIPALMATED SANDPIPER *Calidris pusilla*						
WESTERN SANDPIPER *Calidris mauri*						
SHORT-BILLED DOWITCHER *Limnodromus griseus*						
LONG-BILLED DOWITCHER *Limnodromus scolopaceus*						
JACK SNIPE *Lymnocryptes minimus* (A)						
EURASIAN WOODCOCK *Scolopax rusticola* (A)						
AMERICAN WOODCOCK *Scolopax minor*						
SOLITARY SNIPE *Gallinago solitaria* (A)						
COMMON SNIPE *Gallinago gallinago*						
WILSON'S SNIPE *Gallinago delicata*						
PIN-TAILED SNIPE *Gallinago stenura* (A)						
TEREK SANDPIPER *Xenus cinereus*						
WILSON'S PHALAROPE *Phalaropus tricolor*						
RED-NECKED PHALAROPE *Phalaropus lobatus*						
RED PHALAROPE *Phalaropus fulicarius*						
COMMON SANDPIPER *Actitis hypoleucos*						
SPOTTED SANDPIPER *Actitis macularius*						
GREEN SANDPIPER *Tringa ochropus* (A)						
SOLITARY SANDPIPER *Tringa solitaria*						
GRAY-TAILED TATTLER *Tringa brevipes*						
WANDERING TATTLER *Tringa incana*						
SPOTTED REDSHANK *Tringa erythropus* (A)						
GREATER YELLOWLEGS *Tringa melanoleuca*						
COMMON GREENSHANK *Tringa nebularia*						
WILLET *Tringa semipalmata*						
LESSER YELLOWLEGS *Tringa flavipes*						
MARSH SANDPIPER *Tringa stagnatilis* (A)						

WOOD SANDPIPER *Tringa glareola*							
COMMON REDSHANK *Tringa totanus* (A)							
ORIENTAL PRATINCOLE *Glareola maldivarum* (A)							
GREAT SKUA *Stercorarius skua*							
SOUTH POLAR SKUA *Stercorarius maccormicki*							
POMARINE JAEGER *Stercorarius pomarinus*							
PARASITIC JAEGER *Stercorarius parasiticus*							
LONG-TAILED JAEGER *Stercorarius longicaudus*							
DOVEKIE *Alle alle*							
COMMON MURRE *Uria aalge*							
THICK-BILLED MURRE *Uria lomvia*							
RAZORBILL *Alca torda*							
BLACK GUILLEMOT *Cepphus grylle*							
PIGEON GUILLEMOT *Cepphus columba*							
LONG-BILLED MURRELET *Brachyramphus perdix*							
MARBLED MURRELET *Brachyramphus marmoratus*							
KITTLITZ'S MURRELET *Brachyramphus brevirostris*							
SCRIPPS'S MURRELET *Synthliboramphus scrippsi*							
GUADALUPE MURRELET *Synthliboramphus hypoleucus*							
CRAVERI'S MURRELET *Synthliboramphus craveri*							
ANCIENT MURRELET *Synthliboramphus antiquus*							
CASSIN'S AUKLET *Ptychoramphus aleuticus*							
PARAKEET AUKLET *Aethia psittacula*							
LEAST AUKLET *Aethia pusilla*							
WHISKERED AUKLET *Aethia pygmaea*							
CRESTED AUKLET *Aethia cristatella*							
RHINOCEROS AUKLET *Cerorhinca monocerata*							
ATLANTIC PUFFIN *Fratercula arctica*							
HORNED PUFFIN *Fratercula corniculata*							
TUFTED PUFFIN *Fratercula cirrhata*							

SWALLOW-TAILED GULL *Creagrus furcatus* **(A)**							
BLACK-LEGGED KITTIWAKE *Rissa tridactyla*							
RED-LEGGED KITTIWAKE *Rissa brevirostris*							
IVORY GULL *Pagophila eburnea*							
SABINE'S GULL *Xema sabini*							
BONAPARTE'S GULL *Chroicocephalus philadelphia*							
GRAY-HOODED GULL *Chroicocephalus cirrocephalus* **(A)**							
BLACK-HEADED GULL *Chroicocephalus ridibundus*							
LITTLE GULL *Hydrocoloeus minutus*							
ROSS'S GULL *Rhodostethia rosea*							
LAUGHING GULL *Leucophaeus atricilla*							
FRANKLIN'S GULL *Leucophaeus pipixcan*							
BELCHER'S GULL *Larus belcheri* **(A)**							
BLACK-TAILED GULL *Larus crassirostris* **(A)**							
HEERMANN'S GULL *Larus heermanni*							
MEW GULL *Larus canus*							
RING-BILLED GULL *Larus delawarensis*							
WESTERN GULL *Larus occidentalis*							
YELLOW-FOOTED GULL *Larus livens*							
CALIFORNIA GULL *Larus californicus*							
HERRING GULL *Larus argentatus*							
YELLOW-LEGGED GULL *Larus michahellis* **(A)**							
ICELAND GULL *Larus glaucoides*							
LESSER BLACK-BACKED GULL *Larus fuscus*							
SLATY-BACKED GULL *Larus schistisagus*							
GLAUCOUS-WINGED GULL *Larus glaucescens*							
GLAUCOUS GULL *Larus hyperboreus*							
GREAT BLACK-BACKED GULL *Larus marinus*							
KELP GULL *Larus dominicanus* **(A)**							
BROWN NODDY *Anous stolidus*							

(I) INTRODUCED   (A) ACCIDENTAL   (H) HAWAIIAN

BLACK NODDY *Anous minutus*							
BLUE-GRAY NODDY *Anous ceruleus* (H)							
WHITE TERN *Gygis alba* (H, I)							
SOOTY TERN *Onychoprion fuscatus*							
GRAY-BACKED TERN *Onychoprion lunatus* (H)							
BRIDLED TERN *Onychoprion anaethetus*							
ALEUTIAN TERN *Onychoprion aleuticus*							
LITTLE TERN *Sternula albifrons* (H, A)							
LEAST TERN *Sternula antillarum*							
LARGE-BILLED TERN *Phaetusa simplex* (A)							
GULL-BILLED TERN *Gelochelidon nilotica*							
CASPIAN TERN *Hydroprogne caspia*							
BLACK TERN *Chlidonias niger*							
WHITE-WINGED TERN *Chlidonias leucopterus* (A)							
WHISKERED TERN *Chlidonias hybrida* (A)							
ROSEATE TERN *Sterna dougallii*							
COMMON TERN *Sterna hirundo*							
ARCTIC TERN *Sterna paradisaea*							
FORSTER'S TERN *Sterna forsteri*							
ROYAL TERN *Thalasseus maximus*							
GREAT CRESTED TERN *Thalasseus bergii* (H, A)							
SANDWICH TERN *Thalasseus sandvicensis*							
ELEGANT TERN *Thalasseus elegans*							
BLACK SKIMMER *Rynchops niger*							
PHAETHONTIFORMES							
WHITE-TAILED TROPICBIRD *Phaethon lepturus*							
RED-BILLED TROPICBIRD *Phaethon aethereus*							
RED-TAILED TROPICBIRD *Phaethon rubricauda*							
GAVIIFORMES							
RED-THROATED LOON *Gavia stellata*							

ARCTIC LOON *Gavia arctica*							
PACIFIC LOON *Gavia pacifica*							
COMMON LOON *Gavia immer*							
YELLOW-BILLED LOON *Gavia adamsii*							
PROCELLARIIFORMES							
YELLOW-NOSED ALBATROSS *Thalassarche chlororhynchos* (A)							
WHITE-CAPPED ALBATROSS *Thalassarche cauta* (A)							
SALVIN'S ALBATROSS *Thalassarche salvini* (A)							
CHATHAM ALBATROSS *Thalassarche eremita* (A)							
BLACK-BROWED ALBATROSS *Thalassarche melanophris* (A)							
LIGHT-MANTLED ALBATROSS *Phoebetria palpebrata* (A)							
WANDERING ALBATROSS *Diomedea exulans* (A)							
LAYSAN ALBATROSS *Phoebastria immutabilis*							
BLACK-FOOTED ALBATROSS *Phoebastria nigripes*							
SHORT-TAILED ALBATROSS *Phoebastria albatrus*							
WILSON'S STORM-PETREL *Oceanites oceanicus*							
WHITE-FACED STORM-PETREL *Pelagodroma marina*							
BLACK-BELLIED STORM-PETREL *Fregetta tropica* (A)							
EUROPEAN STORM-PETREL *Hydrobates pelagicus* (A)							
FORK-TAILED STORM-PETREL *Oceanodroma furcata*							
RINGED STORM-PETREL *Oceanodroma hornbyi* (A)							
LEACH'S STORM-PETREL *Oceanodroma leucorhoa*							
TOWNSEND'S STORM-PETREL *Oceanodroma socorroensis*							
SWINHOE'S STORM-PETREL *Oceanodroma monorhis* (A)							
ASHY STORM-PETREL *Oceanodroma homochroa*							
BAND-RUMPED STORM-PETREL *Oceanodroma castro*							
WEDGE-RUMPED STORM-PETREL *Oceanodroma tethys* (A)							
BLACK STORM-PETREL *Oceanodroma melania*							
TRISTRAM'S STORM-PETREL *Oceanodroma tristrami*							
LEAST STORM-PETREL *Oceanodroma microsoma*							

NORTHERN FULMAR *Fulmarus glacialis*							
GRAY-FACED PETREL *Pterodroma gouldi* (A)							
KERMADEC PETREL *Pterodroma neglecta* (A)							
TRINDADE PETREL *Pterodroma arminjoniana*							
HERALD PETREL *Pterodroma heraldica* (H, A)							
MURPHY'S PETREL *Pterodroma ultima*							
PROVIDENCE PETREL *Pterodroma solandri* (A)							
ZINO'S PETREL *Pterodroma madeira* (A)							
FEA'S PETREL *Pterodroma feae*							
MOTTLED PETREL *Pterodroma inexpectata*							
BERMUDA PETREL *Pterodroma cahow*							
BLACK-CAPPED PETREL *Pterodroma hasitata*							
JUAN FERNANDEZ PETREL *Pterodroma externa*							
HAWAIIAN PETREL *Pterodroma sandwichensis*							
WHITE-NECKED PETREL *Pterodroma cervicalis* (H)							
BONIN PETREL *Pterodroma hypoleuca* (H)							
BLACK-WINGED PETREL *Pterodroma nigripennis* (H)							
COOK'S PETREL *Pterodroma cookii*							
STEJNEGER'S PETREL *Pterodroma longirostris* (A)							
BULWER'S PETREL *Bulweria bulwerii*							
JOUANIN'S PETREL *Bulweria fallax* (A)							
TAHITI PETREL *Pseudobulweria rostrata* (H, A)							
WHITE-CHINNED PETREL *Procellaria aequinoctialis* (A)							
PARKINSON'S PETREL *Procellaria parkinsoni* (A)							
STREAKED SHEARWATER *Calonectris leucomelas* (A)							
CORY'S SHEARWATER *Calonectris diomedea*							
CAPE VERDE SHEARWATER *Calonectris edwardsii* (A)							
PINK-FOOTED SHEARWATER *Ardenna creatopus*							
FLESH-FOOTED SHEARWATER *Ardenna carneipes*							
GREAT SHEARWATER *Ardenna gravis*							

WEDGE-TAILED SHEARWATER *Ardenna pacifica*							
BULLER'S SHEARWATER *Ardenna bulleri*							
SOOTY SHEARWATER *Ardenna grisea*							
SHORT-TAILED SHEARWATER *Ardenna tenuirostris*							
CHRISTMAS SHEARWATER *Puffinus nativitatis* (H)							
MANX SHEARWATER *Puffinus puffinus*							
NEWELL'S SHEARWATER *Puffinus newelli*							
BRYAN'S SHEARWATER *Puffinus bryani* (H, A)							
BLACK-VENTED SHEARWATER *Puffinus opisthomelas*							
BAROLO SHEARWATER *Puffinus baroli* (A)							
AUDUBON'S SHEARWATER *Puffinus lherminieri*							
CICONIIFORMES							
JABIRU *Jabiru mycteria* (A)							
WOOD STORK *Mycteria americana*							
SULIFORMES							
LESSER FRIGATEBIRD *Fregata ariel* (A)							
MAGNIFICENT FRIGATEBIRD *Fregata magnificens*							
GREAT FRIGATEBIRD *Fregata minor*							
MASKED BOOBY *Sula dactylatra*							
NAZCA BOOBY *Sula granti* (A)							
BLUE-FOOTED BOOBY *Sula nebouxii* (A)							
BROWN BOOBY *Sula leucogaster*							
RED-FOOTED BOOBY *Sula sula*							
NORTHERN GANNET *Morus bassanus*							
ANHINGA *Anhinga anhinga*							
BRANDT'S CORMORANT *Phalacrocorax penicillatus*							
RED-FACED CORMORANT *Phalacrocorax urile*							
PELAGIC CORMORANT *Phalacrocorax pelagicus*							
GREAT CORMORANT *Phalacrocorax carbo*							
NEOTROPIC CORMORANT *Phalacrocorax brasilianus*							

DOUBLE-CRESTED CORMORANT *Phalacrocorax auritus*								
PELECANIFORMES								
AMERICAN WHITE PELICAN *Pelecanus erythrorhynchos*								
BROWN PELICAN *Pelecanus occidentalis*								
AMERICAN BITTERN *Botaurus lentiginosus*								
YELLOW BITTERN *Ixobrychus sinensis* (A)								
LEAST BITTERN *Ixobrychus exilis*								
BARE-THROATED TIGER-HERON *Tigrisoma mexicanum* (A)								
GREAT BLUE HERON *Ardea herodias*								
GRAY HERON *Ardea cinerea* (A)								
GREAT EGRET *Ardea alba*								
INTERMEDIATE EGRET *Ardea intermedia* (A)								
CHINESE EGRET *Egretta eulophotes* (A)								
LITTLE EGRET *Egretta garzetta* (A)								
WESTERN REEF-HERON *Egretta gularis* (A)								
SNOWY EGRET *Egretta thula*								
LITTLE BLUE HERON *Egretta caerulea*								
TRICOLORED HERON *Egretta tricolor*								
REDDISH EGRET *Egretta rufescens*								
CATTLE EGRET *Bubulcus ibis*								
CHINESE POND-HERON *Ardeola bacchus* (A)								
GREEN HERON *Butorides virescens*								
BLACK-CROWNED NIGHT-HERON *Nycticorax nycticorax*								
YELLOW-CROWNED NIGHT-HERON *Nyctanassa violacea*								
WHITE IBIS *Eudocimus albus*								
SCARLET IBIS *Eudocimus ruber* (A)								
GLOSSY IBIS *Plegadis falcinellus*								
WHITE-FACED IBIS *Plegadis chihi*								
ROSEATE SPOONBILL *Platalea ajaja*								

CHECKLIST
(I) INTRODUCED (A) ACCIDENTAL (H) HAWAIIAN

CATHARTIFORMES

CALIFORNIA CONDOR *Gymnogyps californianus*						
BLACK VULTURE *Coragyps atratus*						
TURKEY VULTURE *Cathartes aura*						

ACCIPITRIFORMES

OSPREY *Pandion haliaetus*						
WHITE-TAILED KITE *Elanus leucurus*						
HOOK-BILLED KITE *Chondrohierax uncinatus*						
SWALLOW-TAILED KITE *Elanoides forficatus*						
GOLDEN EAGLE *Aquila chrysaetos*						
SNAIL KITE *Rostrhamus sociabilis*						
DOUBLE-TOOTHED KITE *Harpagus bidentatus* **(A)**						
MISSISSIPPI KITE *Ictinia mississippiensis*						
NORTHERN HARRIER *Circus hudsonius*						
CHINESE SPARROWHAWK *Accipiter soloensis* **(H, A)**						
SHARP-SHINNED HAWK *Accipiter striatus*						
COOPER'S HAWK *Accipiter cooperii*						
NORTHERN GOSHAWK *Accipiter gentilis*						
BLACK KITE *Milvus migrans* **(A)**						
BALD EAGLE *Haliaeetus leucocephalus*						
WHITE-TAILED EAGLE *Haliaeetus albicilla* **(A)**						
STELLER'S SEA-EAGLE *Haliaeetus pelagicus* **(A)**						
CRANE HAWK *Geranospiza caerulescens* **(A)**						
COMMON BLACK HAWK *Buteogallus anthracinus*						
GREAT BLACK HAWK *Buteogallus urubitinga* **(A)**						
ROADSIDE HAWK *Rupornis magnirostris* **(A)**						
HARRIS'S HAWK *Parabuteo unicinctus*						
WHITE-TAILED HAWK *Geranoaetus albicaudatus*						
GRAY HAWK *Buteo plagiatus*						
RED-SHOULDERED HAWK *Buteo lineatus*						

(I) INTRODUCED (A) ACCIDENTAL (H) HAWAIIAN

BROAD-WINGED HAWK *Buteo platypterus*							
HAWAIIAN HAWK *Buteo solitarius* **(H)**							
SHORT-TAILED HAWK *Buteo brachyurus*							
SWAINSON'S HAWK *Buteo swainsoni*							
ZONE-TAILED HAWK *Buteo albonotatus*							
RED-TAILED HAWK *Buteo jamaicensis*							
ROUGH-LEGGED HAWK *Buteo lagopus*							
FERRUGINOUS HAWK *Buteo regalis*							
STRIGIFORMES							
BARN OWL *Tyto alba*							
ORIENTAL SCOPS-OWL *Otus sunia* **(A)**							
FLAMMULATED OWL *Psiloscops flammeolus*							
WHISKERED SCREECH-OWL *Megascops trichopsis*							
WESTERN SCREECH-OWL *Megascops kennicottii*							
EASTERN SCREECH-OWL *Megascops asio*							
GREAT HORNED OWL *Bubo virginianus*							
SNOWY OWL *Bubo scandiacus*							
NORTHERN HAWK OWL *Surnia ulula*							
NORTHERN PYGMY-OWL *Glaucidium gnoma*							
FERRUGINOUS PYGMY-OWL *Glaucidium brasilianum*							
ELF OWL *Micrathene whitneyi*							
BURROWING OWL *Athene cunicularia*							
MOTTLED OWL *Ciccaba virgata* **(A)**							
SPOTTED OWL *Strix occidentalis*							
BARRED OWL *Strix varia*							
GREAT GRAY OWL *Strix nebulosa*							
LONG-EARED OWL *Asio otus*							
STYGIAN OWL *Asio stygius* **(A)**							
SHORT-EARED OWL *Asio flammeus*							
BOREAL OWL *Aegolius funereus*							

CHECKLIST

(I) INTRODUCED (A) ACCIDENTAL (H) HAWAIIAN

NORTHERN SAW-WHET OWL *Aegolius acadicus*							
NORTHERN BOOBOOK *Ninox japonica* **(A)**							
TROGONIFORMES							
EARED QUETZAL *Euptilotis neoxenus* **(A)**							
ELEGANT TROGON *Trogon elegans*							
BUCEROTIFORMES							
EURASIAN HOOPOE *Upupa epops* **(A)**							
CORACIIFORMES							
RINGED KINGFISHER *Megaceryle torquata*							
BELTED KINGFISHER *Megaceryle alcyon*							
AMAZON KINGFISHER *Chloroceryle amazona* **(A)**							
GREEN KINGFISHER *Chloroceryle americana*							
PICIFORMES							
EURASIAN WRYNECK *Jynx torquilla* **(A)**							
WILLIAMSON'S SAPSUCKER *Sphyrapicus thyroideus*							
YELLOW-BELLIED SAPSUCKER *Sphyrapicus varius*							
RED-NAPED SAPSUCKER *Sphyrapicus nuchalis*							
RED-BREASTED SAPSUCKER *Sphyrapicus ruber*							
LEWIS'S WOODPECKER *Melanerpes lewis*							
RED-HEADED WOODPECKER *Melanerpes erythrocephalus*							
ACORN WOODPECKER *Melanerpes formicivorus*							
GILA WOODPECKER *Melanerpes uropygialis*							
GOLDEN-FRONTED WOODPECKER *Melanerpes aurifrons*							
RED-BELLIED WOODPECKER *Melanerpes carolinus*							
AMERICAN THREE-TOED WOODPECKER *Picoides dorsalis*							
BLACK-BACKED WOODPECKER *Picoides arcticus*							
GREAT SPOTTED WOODPECKER *Dendrocopos major* **(A)**							
DOWNY WOODPECKER *Dryobates pubescens*							
NUTTALL'S WOODPECKER *Dryobates nuttallii*							
LADDER-BACKED WOODPECKER *Dryobates scalaris*							

RED-COCKADED WOODPECKER *Dryobates borealis*							
HAIRY WOODPECKER *Dryobates villosus*							
WHITE-HEADED WOODPECKER *Dryobates albolarvatus*							
ARIZONA WOODPECKER *Dryobates arizonae*							
PILEATED WOODPECKER *Dryocopus pileatus*							
NORTHERN FLICKER *Colaptes auratus*							
GILDED FLICKER *Colaptes chrysoides*							
FALCONIFORMES							
COLLARED FOREST-FALCON *Micrastur semitorquatus* (A)							
CRESTED CARACARA *Caracara cheriway*							
EURASIAN KESTREL *Falco tinnunculus* (A)							
AMERICAN KESTREL *Falco sparverius*							
RED-FOOTED FALCON *Falco vespertinus* (A)							
MERLIN *Falco columbarius*							
EURASIAN HOBBY *Falco subbuteo* (A)							
APLOMADO FALCON *Falco femoralis*							
GYRFALCON *Falco rusticolus*							
PEREGRINE FALCON *Falco peregrinus*							
PRAIRIE FALCON *Falco mexicanus*							
PSITTACIFORMES							
ROSE-RINGED PARAKEET *Psittacula krameri* (H, I)							
ROSY-FACED LOVEBIRD *Agapornis roseicollis* (I)							
MONK PARAKEET *Myiopsitta monachus* (I)							
WHITE-WINGED PARAKEET *Brotogeris versicolurus* (I)							
RED-CROWNED PARROT *Amazona viridigenalis* (I)							
THICK-BILLED PARROT *Rhynchopsitta pachyrhyncha* (Extirpated)							
NANDAY PARAKEET *Aratinga nenday* (I)							
GREEN PARAKEET *Psittacara holochlorus* (I)							
PASSERIFORMES							
NORTHERN BEARDLESS-TYRANNULET *Camptostoma imberbe*							

CHECKLIST
(I) INTRODUCED   (A) ACCIDENTAL   (H) HAWAIIAN

GREENISH ELAENIA *Myiopagis viridicata* **(A)**						
WHITE-CRESTED ELAENIA *Elaenia albiceps* **(A)**						
TUFTED FLYCATCHER *Mitrephanes phaeocercus* **(A)**						
OLIVE-SIDED FLYCATCHER *Contopus cooperi*						
GREATER PEWEE *Contopus pertinax*						
WESTERN WOOD-PEWEE *Contopus sordidulus*						
EASTERN WOOD-PEWEE *Contopus virens*						
CUBAN PEWEE *Contopus caribaeus* **(A)**						
YELLOW-BELLIED FLYCATCHER *Empidonax flaviventris*						
ACADIAN FLYCATCHER *Empidonax virescens*						
ALDER FLYCATCHER *Empidonax alnorum*						
WILLOW FLYCATCHER *Empidonax traillii*						
LEAST FLYCATCHER *Empidonax minimus*						
HAMMOND'S FLYCATCHER *Empidonax hammondii*						
GRAY FLYCATCHER *Empidonax wrightii*						
DUSKY FLYCATCHER *Empidonax oberholseri*						
PINE FLYCATCHER *Empidonax affinis* **(A)**						
PACIFIC-SLOPE FLYCATCHER *Empidonax difficilis*						
CORDILLERAN FLYCATCHER *Empidonax occidentalis*						
BUFF-BREASTED FLYCATCHER *Empidonax fulvifrons*						
BLACK PHOEBE *Sayornis nigricans*						
EASTERN PHOEBE *Sayornis phoebe*						
SAY'S PHOEBE *Sayornis saya*						
VERMILION FLYCATCHER *Pyrocephalus rubinus*						
DUSKY-CAPPED FLYCATCHER *Myiarchus tuberculifer*						
ASH-THROATED FLYCATCHER *Myiarchus cinerascens*						
NUTTING'S FLYCATCHER *Myiarchus nuttingi* **(A)**						
GREAT CRESTED FLYCATCHER *Myiarchus crinitus*						
BROWN-CRESTED FLYCATCHER *Myiarchus tyrannulus*						
LA SAGRA'S FLYCATCHER *Myiarchus sagrae*						

GREAT KISKADEE *Pitangus sulphuratus*							
SOCIAL FLYCATCHER *Myiozetetes similis* (A)							
SULPHUR-BELLIED FLYCATCHER *Myiodynastes luteiventris*							
PIRATIC FLYCATCHER *Legatus leucophaius* (A)							
VARIEGATED FLYCATCHER *Empidonomus varius* (A)							
CROWNED SLATY FLYCATCHER *Empidonomus aurantioatrocristatus* (A)							
TROPICAL KINGBIRD *Tyrannus melancholicus*							
COUCH'S KINGBIRD *Tyrannus couchii*							
CASSIN'S KINGBIRD *Tyrannus vociferans*							
THICK-BILLED KINGBIRD *Tyrannus crassirostris*							
WESTERN KINGBIRD *Tyrannus verticalis*							
EASTERN KINGBIRD *Tyrannus tyrannus*							
GRAY KINGBIRD *Tyrannus dominicensis*							
LOGGERHEAD KINGBIRD *Tyrannus caudifasciatus* (A)							
SCISSOR-TAILED FLYCATCHER *Tyrannus forficatus*							
FORK-TAILED FLYCATCHER *Tyrannus savana*							
MASKED TITYRA *Tityra semifasciata* (A)							
GRAY-COLLARED BECARD *Pachyramphus major* (A)							
ROSE-THROATED BECARD *Pachyramphus aglaiae*							
RED-BACKED SHRIKE *Lanius collurio* (A)							
BROWN SHRIKE *Lanius cristatus* (A)							
LOGGERHEAD SHRIKE *Lanius ludovicianus*							
NORTHERN SHRIKE *Lanius borealis*							
BLACK-CAPPED VIREO *Vireo atricapilla*							
WHITE-EYED VIREO *Vireo griseus*							
THICK-BILLED VIREO *Vireo crassirostris* (A)							
CUBAN VIREO *Vireo gundlachii* (A)							
BELL'S VIREO *Vireo bellii*							
GRAY VIREO *Vireo vicinior*							
HUTTON'S VIREO *Vireo huttoni*							

YELLOW-THROATED VIREO *Vireo flavifrons*							
CASSIN'S VIREO *Vireo cassinii*							
BLUE-HEADED VIREO *Vireo solitarius*							
PLUMBEOUS VIREO *Vireo plumbeus*							
PHILADELPHIA VIREO *Vireo philadelphicus*							
WARBLING VIREO *Vireo gilvus*							
RED-EYED VIREO *Vireo olivaceus*							
YELLOW-GREEN VIREO *Vireo flavoviridis*							
BLACK-WHISKERED VIREO *Vireo altiloquus*							
YUCATAN VIREO *Vireo magister* (A)							
HAWAII ELEPAIO *Chasiempis sandwichensis* (H)							
KAUAI ELEPAIO *Chasiempis sclateri* (H)							
OAHU ELEPAIO *Chasiempis ibidis* (H)							
CANADA JAY *Perisoreus canadensis*							
BROWN JAY *Psilorhinus morio* (A)							
GREEN JAY *Cyanocorax yncas*							
PINYON JAY *Gymnorhinus cyanocephalus*							
STELLER'S JAY *Cyanocitta stelleri*							
BLUE JAY *Cyanocitta cristata*							
FLORIDA SCRUB-JAY *Aphelocoma coerulescens*							
ISLAND SCRUB-JAY *Aphelocoma insularis*							
CALIFORNIA SCRUB-JAY *Aphelocoma californica*							
WOODHOUSE'S SCRUB-JAY *Aphelocoma woodhouseii*							
MEXICAN JAY *Aphelocoma wollweberi*							
BLACK-BILLED MAGPIE *Pica hudsonia*							
YELLOW-BILLED MAGPIE *Pica nuttalli*							
CLARK'S NUTCRACKER *Nucifraga columbiana*							
EURASIAN JACKDAW *Corvus monedula* (A)							
AMERICAN CROW *Corvus brachyrhynchos*							
NORTHWESTERN CROW *Corvus caurinus*							

TAMAULIPAS CROW *Corvus imparatus*						
FISH CROW *Corvus ossifragus*						
HAWAIIAN CROW *Corvus hawaiiensis*						
CHIHUAHUAN RAVEN *Corvus cryptoleucus*						
COMMON RAVEN *Corvus corax*						
HORNED LARK *Eremophila alpestris*						
EURASIAN SKYLARK *Alauda arvensis*						
NORTHERN ROUGH-WINGED SWALLOW *Stelgidopteryx serripennis*						
PURPLE MARTIN *Progne subis*						
CUBAN MARTIN *Progne cryptoleuca* (A)						
GRAY-BREASTED MARTIN *Progne chalybea* (A)						
SOUTHERN MARTIN *Progne elegans* (A)						
BROWN-CHESTED MARTIN *Progne tapera* (A)						
TREE SWALLOW *Tachycineta bicolor*						
MANGROVE SWALLOW *Tachycineta albilinea* (A)						
VIOLET-GREEN SWALLOW *Tachycineta thalassina*						
BAHAMA SWALLOW *Tachycineta cyaneoviridis* (A)						
BANK SWALLOW *Riparia riparia*						
BARN SWALLOW *Hirundo rustica*						
CLIFF SWALLOW *Petrochelidon pyrrhonota*						
CAVE SWALLOW *Petrochelidon fulva*						
COMMON HOUSE-MARTIN *Delichon urbicum* (A)						
CAROLINA CHICKADEE *Poecile carolinensis*						
BLACK-CAPPED CHICKADEE *Poecile atricapillus*						
MOUNTAIN CHICKADEE *Poecile gambeli*						
MEXICAN CHICKADEE *Poecile sclateri*						
CHESTNUT-BACKED CHICKADEE *Poecile rufescens*						
BOREAL CHICKADEE *Poecile hudsonicus*						
GRAY-HEADED CHICKADEE *Poecile cinctus*						
BRIDLED TITMOUSE *Baeolophus wollweberi*						

OAK TITMOUSE *Baeolophus inornatus*								
JUNIPER TITMOUSE *Baeolophus ridgwayi*								
TUFTED TITMOUSE *Baeolophus bicolor*								
BLACK-CRESTED TITMOUSE *Baeolophus atricristatus*								
VERDIN *Auriparus flaviceps*								
BUSHTIT *Psaltriparus minimus*								
RED-BREASTED NUTHATCH *Sitta canadensis*								
WHITE-BREASTED NUTHATCH *Sitta carolinensis*								
PYGMY NUTHATCH *Sitta pygmaea*								
BROWN-HEADED NUTHATCH *Sitta pusilla*								
BROWN CREEPER *Certhia americana*								
ROCK WREN *Salpinctes obsoletus*								
CANYON WREN *Catherpes mexicanus*								
HOUSE WREN *Troglodytes aedon*								
PACIFIC WREN *Troglodytes pacificus*								
WINTER WREN *Troglodytes hiemalis*								
SEDGE WREN *Cistothorus platensis*								
MARSH WREN *Cistothorus palustris*								
CAROLINA WREN *Thryothorus ludovicianus*								
BEWICK'S WREN *Thryomanes bewickii*								
CACTUS WREN *Campylorhynchus brunneicapillus*								
SINALOA WREN *Thryophilus sinaloa* (A)								
BLUE-GRAY GNATCATCHER *Polioptila caerulea*								
CALIFORNIA GNATCATCHER *Polioptila californica*								
BLACK-TAILED GNATCATCHER *Polioptila melanura*								
BLACK-CAPPED GNATCATCHER *Polioptila nigriceps*								
AMERICAN DIPPER *Cinclus mexicanus*								
RED-VENTED BULBUL *Pycnonotus cafer* (H, I)								
RED-WHISKERED BULBUL *Pycnonotus jocosus* (I)								
GOLDEN-CROWNED KINGLET *Regulus satrapa*								

RUBY-CROWNED KINGLET *Regulus calendula*							
JAPANESE BUSH WARBLER *Horornis diphone* (H, I)							
WOOD WARBLER *Phylloscopus sibilatrix* (A)							
YELLOW-BROWED WARBLER *Phylloscopus inornatus* (A)							
PALLAS'S LEAF WARBLER *Phylloscopus proregulus* (A)							
DUSKY WARBLER *Phylloscopus fuscatus* (A)							
WILLOW WARBLER *Phylloscopus trochilus* (A)							
COMMON CHIFFCHAFF *Phylloscopus collybita* (A)							
ARCTIC WARBLER *Phylloscopus borealis*							
KAMCHATKA LEAF WARBLER *Phylloscopus examinandus* (A)							
THICK-BILLED WARBLER *Arundinax aedon* (A)							
SEDGE WARBLER *Acrocephalus schoenobaenus* (A)							
BLYTH'S REED WARBLER *Acrocephalus dumetorum* (A)							
MILLERBIRD *Acrocephalus familiaris* (H)							
MIDDENDORFF'S GRASSHOPPER-WARBLER *Locustella ochotensis* (A)							
LANCEOLATED WARBLER *Locustella lanceolata* (A)							
EURASIAN RIVER WARBLER *Locustella fluviatilis* (A)							
LESSER WHITETHROAT *Sylvia curruca* (A)							
WRENTIT *Chamaea fasciata*							
JAPANESE WHITE-EYE *Zosterops japonicus* (H, I)							
CHINESE HWAMEI *Garrulax canorus* (H, I)							
GREATER NECKLACED LAUGHINGTHRUSH *Ianthocincla pectoralis* (H, I)							
RED-BILLED LEIOTHRIX *Leiothrix lutea* (H, I)							
GRAY-STREAKED FLYCATCHER *Muscicapa griseisticta* (A)							
DARK-SIDED FLYCATCHER *Muscicapa sibirica* (A)							
ASIAN BROWN FLYCATCHER *Muscicapa dauurica* (A)							
SPOTTED FLYCATCHER *Muscicapa striata* (A)							
WHITE-RUMPED SHAMA *Copsychus malabaricus* (H)							
EUROPEAN ROBIN *Erithacus rubecula* (A)							
RUFOUS-TAILED ROBIN *Larvivora sibilans* (A)							

CHECKLIST
(I) INTRODUCED   (A) ACCIDENTAL   (H) HAWAIIAN

SIBERIAN BLUE ROBIN *Larvivora cyane* (A)						
BLUETHROAT *Luscinia svecica*						
SIBERIAN RUBYTHROAT *Calliope calliope*						
RED-FLANKED BLUETAIL *Tarsiger cyanurus* (A)						
NARCISSUS FLYCATCHER *Ficedula narcissina* (A)						
MUGIMAKI FLYCATCHER *Ficedula mugimaki* (A)						
TAIGA FLYCATCHER *Ficedula albicilla* (A)						
COMMON REDSTART *Phoenicurus phoenicurus* (A)						
SIBERIAN STONECHAT *Saxicola maurus* (A)						
NORTHERN WHEATEAR *Oenanthe oenanthe*						
PIED WHEATEAR *Oenanthe pleschanka* (A)						
EASTERN BLUEBIRD *Sialia sialis*						
WESTERN BLUEBIRD *Sialia mexicana*						
MOUNTAIN BLUEBIRD *Sialia currucoides*						
TOWNSEND'S SOLITAIRE *Myadestes townsendi*						
BROWN-BACKED SOLITAIRE *Myadestes occidentalis* (A)						
OMAO *Myadestes obscurus* (H)						
PUAIOHI *Myadestes palmeri* (H)						
VARIED THRUSH *Ixoreus naevius*						
ORANGE-BILLED NIGHTINGALE-THRUSH *Catharus aurantiirostris* (A)						
BLACK-HEADED NIGHTINGALE-THRUSH *Catharus mexicanus* (A)						
VEERY *Catharus fuscescens*						
GRAY-CHEEKED THRUSH *Catharus minimus*						
BICKNELL'S THRUSH *Catharus bicknelli*						
SWAINSON'S THRUSH *Catharus ustulatus*						
HERMIT THRUSH *Catharus guttatus*						
WOOD THRUSH *Hylocichla mustelina*						
AZTEC THRUSH *Ridgwayia pinicola* (A)						
MISTLE THRUSH *Turdus viscivorus* (A)						
SONG THRUSH *Turdus philomelos* (A)						

CHECKLIST
(I) INTRODUCED   (A) ACCIDENTAL   (H) HAWAIIAN

REDWING *Turdus iliacus* (A)							
EURASIAN BLACKBIRD *Turdus merula* (A)							
WHITE-THROATED THRUSH *Turdus assimilis* (A)							
CLAY-COLORED THRUSH *Turdus grayi*							
AMERICAN ROBIN *Turdus migratorius*							
RUFOUS-BACKED ROBIN *Turdus rufopalliatus*							
RED-LEGGED THRUSH *Turdus plumbeus* (A)							
EYEBROWED THRUSH *Turdus obscurus*							
FIELDFARE *Turdus pilaris* (A)							
DUSKY THRUSH *Turdus eunomus* (A)							
NAUMANN'S THRUSH *Turdus naumanni* (A)							
BLUE MOCKINGBIRD *Melanotis caerulescens* (A)							
GRAY CATBIRD *Dumetella carolinensis*							
CURVE-BILLED THRASHER *Toxostoma curvirostre*							
BROWN THRASHER *Toxostoma rufum*							
LONG-BILLED THRASHER *Toxostoma longirostre*							
BENDIRE'S THRASHER *Toxostoma bendirei*							
CALIFORNIA THRASHER *Toxostoma redivivum*							
LECONTE'S THRASHER *Toxostoma lecontei*							
CRISSAL THRASHER *Toxostoma crissale*							
SAGE THRASHER *Oreoscoptes montanus*							
BAHAMA MOCKINGBIRD *Mimus gundlachii* (A)							
NORTHERN MOCKINGBIRD *Mimus polyglottos*							
EUROPEAN STARLING *Sturnus vulgaris* (I) (A)							
COMMON MYNA *Acridotheres tristis* (I)							
SIBERIAN ACCENTOR *Prunella montanella* (A)							
GRAY WAGTAIL *Motacilla cinerea* (A)							
EASTERN YELLOW WAGTAIL *Motacilla tschutschensis*							
CITRINE WAGTAIL *Motacilla citreola* (A)							
WHITE WAGTAIL *Motacilla alba*							

(I) INTRODUCED   (A) ACCIDENTAL   (H) HAWAIIAN

TREE PIPIT *Anthus trivialis* (A)								
OLIVE-BACKED PIPIT *Anthus hodgsoni*								
PECHORA PIPIT *Anthus gustavi* (A)								
RED-THROATED PIPIT *Anthus cervinus*								
AMERICAN PIPIT *Anthus rubescens*								
SPRAGUE'S PIPIT *Anthus spragueii*								
BOHEMIAN WAXWING *Bombycilla garrulus*								
CEDAR WAXWING *Bombycilla cedrorum*								
GRAY SILKY-FLYCATCHER *Ptiliogonys cinereus* (A)								
PHAINOPEPLA *Phainopepla nitens*								
OLIVE WARBLER *Peucedramus taeniatus*								
COMMON CHAFFINCH *Fringilla coelebs* (A)								
BRAMBLING *Fringilla montifringilla*								
EVENING GROSBEAK *Coccothraustes vespertinus*								
HAWFINCH *Coccothraustes coccothraustes* (A)								
AKIKIKI *Oreomystis bairdi* (H)								
MAUI ALAUAHIO *Paroreomyza montana* (H)								
PALILA *Loxioides bailleui* (H)								
LAYSAN FINCH *Telespiza cantans* (H)								
NIHOA FINCH *Telespiza ultima* (H)								
AKOHEKOHE *Palmeria dolei* (H)								
APAPANE *Himatione sanguinea* (H)								
IIWI *Drepanis coccinea* (H)								
MAUI PARROTBILL *Pseudonestor xanthophrys* (H)								
AKIAPOLAAU *Hemignathus wilsoni* (H)								
ANIANIAU *Magumma parva* (H)								
HAWAII AMAKIHI *Chlorodrepanis virens* (H)								
OAHU AMAKIHI *Chlorodrepanis flava* (H)								
KAUAI AMAKIHI *Chlorodrepanis stejnegeri* (H)								
HAWAII CREEPER *Loxops mana* (H)								

AKEKEE *Loxops caeruleirostris* **(H)**							
HAWAII AKEPA *Loxops coccineus* **(H)**							
COMMON ROSEFINCH *Carpodacus erythrinus* **(A)**							
PALLAS'S ROSEFINCH *Carpodacus roseus* **(A)**							
PINE GROSBEAK *Pinicola enucleator*							
EURASIAN BULLFINCH *Pyrrhula pyrrhula* **(A)**							
ASIAN ROSY-FINCH *Leucosticte arctoa* **(A)**							
GRAY-CROWNED ROSY-FINCH *Leucosticte tephrocotis*							
BLACK ROSY-FINCH *Leucosticte atrata*							
BROWN-CAPPED ROSY-FINCH *Leucosticte australis*							
HOUSE FINCH *Haemorhous mexicanus*							
PURPLE FINCH *Haemorhous purpureus*							
CASSIN'S FINCH *Haemorhous cassinii*							
ORIENTAL GREENFINCH *Chloris sinica* **(A)**							
YELLOW-FRONTED CANARY *Crithagra mozambica* **(H, I)**							
COMMON REDPOLL *Acanthis flammea*							
HOARY REDPOLL *Acanthis hornemanni*							
RED CROSSBILL *Loxia curvirostra*							
CASSIA CROSSBILL *Loxia sinesciuris*							
WHITE-WINGED CROSSBILL *Loxia leucoptera*							
ISLAND CANARY *Serinus canaria* **(H, I)**							
EURASIAN SISKIN *Spinus spinus* **(A)**							
PINE SISKIN *Spinus pinus*							
LESSER GOLDFINCH *Spinus psaltria*							
LAWRENCE'S GOLDFINCH *Spinus lawrencei*							
AMERICAN GOLDFINCH *Spinus tristis*							
LAPLAND LONGSPUR *Calcarius lapponicus*							
CHESTNUT-COLLARED LONGSPUR *Calcarius ornatus*							
SMITH'S LONGSPUR *Calcarius pictus*							
MCCOWN'S LONGSPUR *Rhynchophanes mccownii*							

CHECKLIST

(I) INTRODUCED (A) ACCIDENTAL (H) HAWAIIAN

SNOW BUNTING *Plectrophenax nivalis*							
MCKAY'S BUNTING *Plectrophenax hyperboreus*							
PINE BUNTING *Emberiza leucocephalos* (A)							
YELLOW-THROATED BUNTING *Emberiza elegans* (A)							
PALLAS'S BUNTING *Emberiza pallasi* (A)							
REED BUNTING *Emberiza schoeniclus* (A)							
YELLOW-BREASTED BUNTING *Emberiza aureola* (A)							
LITTLE BUNTING *Emberiza pusilla* (A)							
RUSTIC BUNTING *Emberiza rustica*							
YELLOW-BROWED BUNTING *Emberiza chrysophrys* (A)							
GRAY BUNTING *Emberiza variabilis* (A)							
RUFOUS-WINGED SPARROW *Peucaea carpalis*							
BOTTERI'S SPARROW *Peucaea botterii*							
CASSIN'S SPARROW *Peucaea cassinii*							
BACHMAN'S SPARROW *Peucaea aestivalis*							
GRASSHOPPER SPARROW *Ammodramus savannarum*							
OLIVE SPARROW *Arremonops rufivirgatus*							
CHIPPING SPARROW *Spizella passerina*							
CLAY-COLORED SPARROW *Spizella pallida*							
BLACK-CHINNED SPARROW *Spizella atrogularis*							
FIELD SPARROW *Spizella pusilla*							
BREWER'S SPARROW *Spizella breweri*							
WORTHEN'S SPARROW *Spizella wortheni* (A)							
BLACK-THROATED SPARROW *Amphispiza bilineata*							
FIVE-STRIPED SPARROW *Amphispiza quinquestriata*							
LARK SPARROW *Chondestes grammacus*							
LARK BUNTING *Calamospiza melanocorys*							
AMERICAN TREE SPARROW *Spizelloides arborea*							
FOX SPARROW *Passerella iliaca*							
DARK-EYED JUNCO *Junco hyemalis*							

YELLOW-EYED JUNCO *Junco phaeonotus*							
WHITE-CROWNED SPARROW *Zonotrichia leucophrys*							
GOLDEN-CROWNED SPARROW *Zonotrichia atricapilla*							
HARRIS'S SPARROW *Zonotrichia querula*							
WHITE-THROATED SPARROW *Zonotrichia albicollis*							
SAGEBRUSH SPARROW *Artemisiospiza nevadensis*							
BELL'S SPARROW *Artemisiospiza belli*							
VESPER SPARROW *Pooecetes gramineus*							
LECONTE'S SPARROW *Ammospiza leconteii*							
SEASIDE SPARROW *Ammospiza maritima*							
NELSON'S SPARROW *Ammospiza nelsoni*							
SALTMARSH SPARROW *Ammospiza caudacuta*							
SAVANNAH SPARROW *Passerculus sandwichensis*							
BAIRD'S SPARROW *Centronyx bairdii*							
HENSLOW'S SPARROW *Centronyx henslowii*							
SONG SPARROW *Melospiza melodia*							
LINCOLN'S SPARROW *Melospiza lincolnii*							
SWAMP SPARROW *Melospiza georgiana*							
CANYON TOWHEE *Melozone fusca*							
ABERT'S TOWHEE *Melozone aberti*							
CALIFORNIA TOWHEE *Melozone crissalis*							
RUFOUS-CROWNED SPARROW *Aimophila ruficeps*							
GREEN-TAILED TOWHEE *Pipilo chlorurus*							
SPOTTED TOWHEE *Pipilo maculatus*							
EASTERN TOWHEE *Pipilo erythrophthalmus*							
WESTERN SPINDALIS *Spindalis zena*							
YELLOW-BREASTED CHAT *Icteria virens*							
YELLOW-HEADED BLACKBIRD *Xanthocephalus xanthocephalus*							
BOBOLINK *Dolichonyx oryzivorus*							
WESTERN MEADOWLARK *Sturnella neglecta*							

EASTERN MEADOWLARK *Sturnella magna*							
BLACK-VENTED ORIOLE *Icterus wagleri* (A)							
ORCHARD ORIOLE *Icterus spurius*							
HOODED ORIOLE *Icterus cucullatus*							
STREAK-BACKED ORIOLE *Icterus pustulatus* (A)							
BULLOCK'S ORIOLE *Icterus bullockii*							
SPOT-BREASTED ORIOLE *Icterus pectoralis* (I)							
ALTAMIRA ORIOLE *Icterus gularis*							
AUDUBON'S ORIOLE *Icterus graduacauda*							
BALTIMORE ORIOLE *Icterus galbula*							
BLACK-BACKED ORIOLE *Icterus abeillei* (A)							
SCOTT'S ORIOLE *Icterus parisorum*							
RED-WINGED BLACKBIRD *Agelaius phoeniceus*							
TRICOLORED BLACKBIRD *Agelaius tricolor*							
TAWNY-SHOULDERED BLACKBIRD *Agelaius humeralis* (A)							
SHINY COWBIRD *Molothrus bonariensis*							
BRONZED COWBIRD *Molothrus aeneus*							
BROWN-HEADED COWBIRD *Molothrus ater*							
RUSTY BLACKBIRD *Euphagus carolinus*							
BREWER'S BLACKBIRD *Euphagus cyanocephalus*							
COMMON GRACKLE *Quiscalus quiscula*							
BOAT-TAILED GRACKLE *Quiscalus major*							
GREAT-TAILED GRACKLE *Quiscalus mexicanus*							
OVENBIRD *Seiurus aurocapilla*							
WORM-EATING WARBLER *Helmitheros vermivorum*							
LOUISIANA WATERTHRUSH *Parkesia motacilla*							
NORTHERN WATERTHRUSH *Parkesia noveboracensis*							
GOLDEN-WINGED WARBLER *Vermivora chrysoptera*							
BLUE-WINGED WARBLER *Vermivora cyanoptera*							
BLACK-AND-WHITE WARBLER *Mniotilta varia*							

CHECKLIST
(I) INTRODUCED (A) ACCIDENTAL (H) HAWAIIAN

PROTHONOTARY WARBLER *Protonotaria citrea*							
SWAINSON'S WARBLER *Limnothlypis swainsonii*							
CRESCENT-CHESTED WARBLER *Oreothlypis superciliosa* (A)							
TENNESSEE WARBLER *Oreothlypis peregrina*							
ORANGE-CROWNED WARBLER *Oreothlypis celata*							
COLIMA WARBLER *Oreothlypis crissalis*							
LUCY'S WARBLER *Oreothlypis luciae*							
NASHVILLE WARBLER *Oreothlypis ruficapilla*							
VIRGINIA'S WARBLER *Oreothlypis virginiae*							
CONNECTICUT WARBLER *Oporornis agilis*							
GRAY-CROWNED YELLOWTHROAT *Geothlypis poliocephala* (A)							
MACGILLIVRAY'S WARBLER *Geothlypis tolmiei*							
MOURNING WARBLER *Geothlypis philadelphia*							
KENTUCKY WARBLER *Geothlypis formosa*							
COMMON YELLOWTHROAT *Geothlypis trichas*							
HOODED WARBLER *Setophaga citrina*							
AMERICAN REDSTART *Setophaga ruticilla*							
KIRTLAND'S WARBLER *Setophaga kirtlandii*							
CAPE MAY WARBLER *Setophaga tigrina*							
CERULEAN WARBLER *Setophaga cerulea*							
NORTHERN PARULA *Setophaga americana*							
TROPICAL PARULA *Setophaga pitiayumi*							
MAGNOLIA WARBLER *Setophaga magnolia*							
BAY-BREASTED WARBLER *Setophaga castanea*							
BLACKBURNIAN WARBLER *Setophaga fusca*							
YELLOW WARBLER *Setophaga petechia*							
CHESTNUT-SIDED WARBLER *Setophaga pensylvanica*							
BLACKPOLL WARBLER *Setophaga striata*							
BLACK-THROATED BLUE WARBLER *Setophaga caerulescens*							
PALM WARBLER *Setophaga palmarum*							

PINE WARBLER *Setophaga pinus*							
YELLOW-RUMPED WARBLER *Setophaga coronata*							
YELLOW-THROATED WARBLER *Setophaga dominica*							
PRAIRIE WARBLER *Setophaga discolor*							
GRACE'S WARBLER *Setophaga graciae*							
BLACK-THROATED GRAY WARBLER *Setophaga nigrescens*							
TOWNSEND'S WARBLER *Setophaga townsendi*							
HERMIT WARBLER *Setophaga occidentalis*							
GOLDEN-CHEEKED WARBLER *Setophaga chrysoparia*							
BLACK-THROATED GREEN WARBLER *Setophaga virens*							
FAN-TAILED WARBLER *Basileuterus lachrymosus* (A)							
RUFOUS-CAPPED WARBLER *Basileuterus rufifrons*							
GOLDEN-CROWNED WARBLER *Basileuterus culicivorus* (A)							
CANADA WARBLER *Cardellina canadensis*							
WILSON'S WARBLER *Cardellina pusilla*							
RED-FACED WARBLER *Cardellina rubrifrons*							
PAINTED REDSTART *Myioborus pictus*							
SLATE-THROATED REDSTART *Myioborus miniatus* (A)							
HEPATIC TANAGER *Piranga flava*							
SUMMER TANAGER *Piranga rubra*							
SCARLET TANAGER *Piranga olivacea*							
WESTERN TANAGER *Piranga ludoviciana*							
FLAME-COLORED TANAGER *Piranga bidentata*							
CRIMSON-COLLARED GROSBEAK *Rhodothraupis celaeno* (A)							
NORTHERN CARDINAL *Cardinalis cardinalis*							
PYRRHULOXIA *Cardinalis sinuatus*							
YELLOW GROSBEAK *Pheucticus chrysopeplus* (A)							
ROSE-BREASTED GROSBEAK *Pheucticus ludovicianus*							
BLACK-HEADED GROSBEAK *Pheucticus melanocephalus*							
BLUE BUNTING *Cyanocompsa parellina* (A)							

BLUE GROSBEAK *Passerina caerulea*								
LAZULI BUNTING *Passerina amoena*								
INDIGO BUNTING *Passerina cyanea*								
VARIED BUNTING *Passerina versicolor*								
PAINTED BUNTING *Passerina ciris*								
DICKCISSEL *Spiza americana*								
RED-CRESTED CARDINAL *Paroaria coronata* (H, I)								
YELLOW-BILLED CARDINAL *Paroaria capitata* (H, I)								
RED-LEGGED HONEYCREEPER *Cyanerpes cyaneus* (A)								
SAFFRON FINCH *Sicalis flaveola* (H, I)								
MORELET'S SEEDEATER *Sporophila morelleti*								
BANANAQUIT *Coereba flaveola* (A)								
YELLOW-FACED GRASSQUIT *Tiaris olivaceus* (A) (H, I)								
BLACK-FACED GRASSQUIT *Tiaris bicolor* (A)								
HOUSE SPARROW *Passer domesticus* (I)								
EURASIAN TREE SPARROW *Passer montanus* (I)								
COMMON WAXBILL *Estrilda astrild* (H, I)								
RED AVADAVAT *Amandava amandava* (H, I)								
AFRICAN SILVERBILL *Euodice cantans* (H, I)								
SCALY-BREASTED MUNIA *Lonchura punctulata* (I)								
CHESTNUT MUNIA *Lonchura atricapilla* (H, I)								
JAVA SPARROW *Lonchura oryzivora* (H, I)								

Common
Grackles

Date: Location:

Date: Location:

Date: Location:

Date: Location:

Date: Location:

Date: Location:

Date: Location:

Date: Location:

Date: Location:

Date: Location:

BIRD NOTES

Date: Location:

Date: Location:

Date: Location:

Date: Location:

Date: Location:

Date: Location:

Date: Location:

Date: Location:

Date: Location:

Date: Location:

Date: Location:

Date: Location:

Date: Location:

Date: Location:

Date:	Location:

Date: Location:

Date:	Location:

Date: Location:

Date:	Location:

Date: Location:

Date:	Location:

Date: Location:

Date: Location:

Date: Location:

Date:	Location:

Date: Location:

Date:

Location:

*Rose-breasted
Grosbeaks*

Y

ACKNOWLEDGMENTS

This latest edition was put together with the help of many people. Marshall Iliff provided guidance on the checklist, Kevin McGowan and Lee Ann van Leer gave feedback on format, Chris Farmer assisted with the list of extinct Hawaiian birds, Rachel Lodder enthusiastically proofread several versions of the list, Rigel Stuhmiller's buoyant illustrations and Patricia Mitter's inspired design gave it a fresh look, and Jill Leichter guided this project from concept to publication. Last, but certainly not least, we would like to thank the eBird community for their observations. Their contributions to eBird benefit scientific research and conservation, and provide us with a more complete understanding of the distribution of birds, including accidental species.

Tufted Titmouse